CW00493148

LITTLE TYKE

LITTLE TYKE

Memories of a Yorkshire Childhood
and
Farewell to Yorkshire

by

D AVID C. F ANTHORPE

The Memoir Club

© David C. Fanthorpe 2009

First published in 2009 by
The Memoir Club
Arya House
Langley Park
Durham
DH7 9XE

British Library Cataloguing in
Publication Data.
A catalogue record for this book
is available from the
British Library

ISBN: 978-1-84104-195-7

Typeset by TW Typesetting, Plymouth, Devon
Printed in Great Britain by the MPG Books Group, Bodmin and King's Lynn

For
Ben, Luke, Joe and Ella

Contents

Book I Memories of a Yorkshire Childhood

Book II Farewell to Yorkshire

List of Illustrations

Acknowledgements

I am greatly indebted to Ralph Windle (alias Bertie Ramsbottom) for allowing me to use lines from his amazingly insightful book *The Bottom Line, A Book of Business Ballads*, Century Publishing. I use them in homage to his poetic and business genius. It is only his unique talent that could possibly describe the intimate and sometimes scurrilous workings of industry and business not only with excruciatingly erudite and wicked wit, but in poetry!

I am likewise deeply indebted to publishers John Wiley and Sons, Inc. for allowing quotations from *Up the Organization by* the late Robert Townsend (*Up the Organization: How to stop the company stifling people and strangling profits*). I use them, as I used his book widely in business life, to illuminate the paths of business and to tell me how to do it right. The wit of his writing is only matched by the brilliance of his business acumen. Thank heavens for a publisher who keeps a timeless gem of business wisdom in print thirty-eight years after it was first published!

(I once gave a paper for the Department of Trade and Industry at a Conference they had organized on Best Management Practice. At the end of my delivery I invited questions from the audience. The first question was 'Which business books did I recommend they should all go away and read?' I told them without hesitation and with only a small tongue in cheek that the only two books they ever need read were *The Bottom Line – A Book of Business Ballads* by Bertie Ramsbottom and *Up the Organization* by Robert Townsend. After them, all the rest would seem pompous, dreary and superfluous. Years later, I met some attendees. I got no complaints on my recommendations.)

Thanks must go to the publishers of *Management Today,* Haymarket Business Media, for permission to use their heading and photograph from their September 1988 feature article on Britain's Best Factories. I always found *Management Today* to be an august and authoritative magazine much admired and trusted by all the businessmen I ever met.

I must also give grateful thanks to my brothers Douglas and Michael Fanthorpe and to my nephew David M. Pflasterer for trusting me with their precious, ancient family photographs, and for their thoughtful additions and corrections to my memory of events. I am also grateful for their trust and forbearance in allowing me to put them into print as part of my story and for their comments which improved the finished product. I am forever grateful for their encouragements.

Introduction

The fog of memory

I remember some parts of my childhood quite vividly, but the fog of indistinct memory increases as you get older and the certainties of youthful memory get blurred until you start to ask, 'Was it really like that?' My generation and that of my father were not diverted by such things. Indeed, to be too bothered at all about your ancestry let alone its intimate characteristics was considered a frippery and an affectation of the upper classes, 'the Tory vermin' as Aneurin Bevan put it, in the dour working class Yorkshire society I was born into. But times change. Many of my now made good contemporaries have said to me how they wished they had sat down with their parents and discovered what their story was from their perspective, and for that matter what was their grandparents' story. In case my children, the grandchildren I now know and those I don't yet know, ever have the same maturing regret, I thought I should put down what I remember of my life, my history and my family's history before the fog completely obliterates factual memory and replaces it with the fond or bitter illusions of old age. It is, of course, a story from my perspective and sometimes it is surmise, as impressions of others, even intimate family members, have to be because of the reluctance all people have about revealing themselves as they truly are. But then, isn't my perspective that which makes me what I am? If sometime in the future anyone has even a passing fancy to know 'what was the cantankerous old bugger really like and why was he like that?' or 'what were those early and mid twentieth century times really like?', then I hope this will help them understand that it was the times and all that happened in them that made me, and for that matter many others, the way we are.

I may be a cantankerous old bugger now – no, this is supposed to be truthful – I have always been opinionated, loud and argumentative and as you get older and your opinions get less relevant to the younger generation, this amounts to cantankerous, but I have always loved rational words ever since I discovered John Steinbeck whose writing is as close to painfully truthful of the human condition as I have ever found. And then, I am a sucker for the whimsical and the even viciously funny. Yes, I have laughed a lot as well.

I will try to be scrupulously honest in what I tell you of my life. But here and there will be not so much black lies, more like some half truths. Some things can only cause pain without the benefit of enlightening my story in any way. If you catch me out in one of these small half truths sometime in the future, you will then almost certainly know the reason for my evasion and by knowing, you will almost certainly forgive me. Or at least, that is my hope.

> If you look deeply into the palm of your hand, you will see your parents and all generations of your ancestors. All of them are alive in this moment. Each is present in your body. You are the continuation of each of these people.
>
> Thich Nhat Hanh
> Vietnamese monk, activist and writer

Book I

Memories of a Yorkshire Childhood

CHAPTER 1

An industrial Yorkshire childhood – Little Tykes

And was Jerusalem builded here
Among those dark Satanic Mills?

William Blake: 'Jerusalem'

I WAS BORN ON SUNDAY 22 March 1942 at about 4.00 in the afternoon. I know this because my mother told me so. She remembered the time because, according to her, *Music While You Work* was on the BBC Home Service at the time. I think the irony of *Music While You Work* playing while she was in her great labour was totally lost on her, but it always struck me as funny. And it was a great labour. Apparently, when the midwife weighed me on her spring balance, which only reached 12 pounds maximum, the machine reached its limit so I was recorded at 'about 12 pounds'. 1942 was the height of the War so how my mother came to produce such a monster on the meagre rations of those years remains a mystery. *Music While You Work* was part of the BBC's War effort in helping The Workers maintain their morale while maximising their production for the War Effort, which is why, I have always presumed, *Music While You Work* was playing on a Sunday afternoon, there being no rest for the home front while the War was being waged by our soldiers and sailors out in Europe and the oceans of the world.

My father certainly took his production targets seriously. I was the fifth child of the brood, though at the time (or at least when I was able to comprehend such things) I thought I was the fourth. There was Douglas, the eldest of the family and the golden boy on whom all parental hope lay. He was fourteen years older than me. Then there was Dorothy, nine years older, and Marguerite, four years older. Then me, quite clearly the fourth. What I didn't know was that there had been another daughter, Pauline, who had come between Dorothy and Marguerite. She had died of diphtheria two years before I was born, and my mother would never speak of her so it was many years before I gradually became aware of her and the

3

terrible guilt my mother felt at her loss. When Pauline was born in June 1935 the burden of a third child, on what must have been a savagely stretched budget in the thirties Depression years (judging by the poverty that blessed my childhood), had been decided intolerable, probably by my father, and Pauline was given away to Charlie, my father's brother, and his wife Florrie who were childless at that time and desperate for children. They lived in Worksop about twenty miles from Doncaster, but in those days twenty miles might as well have been a thousand. Pauline caught diphtheria and died in Worksop aged five in November 1940. My mother blamed herself that Pauline was in Worksop to catch diphtheria and that she wasn't there to save her. She carried this great sadness and guilt all her life to the grave and it must have been the original source of the great corrosive bitterness with which her life became blighted.

My mother told me in later years that Father, being the fundamentalist he was in all things, insisted I was breast fed as all my predecessors had been. But she had no milk, probably as a result of the diet of the War years and as a consequence of having five children. So I went hungry and cried an awful lot and it was many weeks before my father would relent and allow bottle feeding, and then only because there was no peace in the house with my bawling. What a good job I had been born so big, I have since thought, or I would surely have died from malnutrition or disease in my infancy while Father pursued his fundamentalist dictatorship over women.

I was born and lived those early years in the back streets of Balby, all named after famous poets (I think now that I know him better that Lord Byron would have been appalled to have lent his name to those streets), in Doncaster, mostly defined then by railways and King Coal as a town. I'm still irrationally proud of the fact that Mallard, the fastest steam train ever, and the Flying Scotsman, the most romantic, were built in the Plant Works, Doncaster by Sir Nigel Gresley for the LNER.

Our house was part of a terrace, still there to this day, in what was then a roughish working class neighbourhood which my mother hated because of some of the colourful and vulgarly noisy neighbours. One of the things that characterised her was her refusal to accept her station in life, as you were required to do in those days. Good for her! She always had delusions of grandeur which, largely unfulfilled, helped fuel her later bile. It was a small council house with, I think, three small bedrooms and two rooms downstairs and only an outside lavatory which froze solid in winter and was fed with torn up sheets of the *Daily Herald*, the only socialist newspaper allowed in the house. It gave me immense satisfaction in later life to remember that I had wiped my backside on the main socialist organ of the day, but that was much later after my conversion to 'the vermin'. On the other hand the socialists, if they only knew, had managed to imprint their dogma on the most intimate part of my anatomy which only my mother would normally have reluctant access to. Newspaper, especially the coarse wartime stuff, did not make for the best bum paper, and given that all children seem to use twenty times more than adults anyway (I have noticed this in my grandchildren, much to my chagrin when I have to plunge our loos) I frequently totally blocked the privy. Poor old Dad would have to clear it when he came home tired from his shift. I can still hear him now: 'Bloody hell, Kathy [my mother], those kids must have backsides like elephants.'

It was an extremely cold house in winter, as indeed most houses were. There was only one source of heat downstairs, one of those wonderful black-leaded ranges that included the boiler for hot water and the oven for cooking. Huddled around it in winter your front would be scorched until it went blotchy, the colour and pattern of corned beef, and your back would be almost literally freezing. The window panes even in this warmest room in the house would freeze up overnight on the inside with wonderful frost patterns. Upstairs there was one fireplace in my parents' bedroom, but this was never lit except in the event of serious sickness in the house. Upstairs was Jack Frost's kingdom in winter, frozen solid it seemed to me from November through to March. We slept with the full quota of blankets and army surplus greatcoats, Billy Connolly style, having got undressed downstairs in front of the great black-leaded range and put on our raggy pyjamas taken from the range oven deliciously warm. Once we had scurried as quickly as possible over the stinging linoleum and dived into bed we daren't move under the pile of greatcoats because to move would be to feel the cold. When I grew a little older we would all warm house bricks in the oven, wrap them in old sheets and use them in place of water bottles in bed.

The gardens to front and rear were privet hedged and all turned over to vegetable production as was required of all householders in the War. I think now that my love of fresh vegetables was born in those gardens, for it seems to me that they were beyond delicious, those potatoes (Arran Pilots I remember), broad beans (Windsors) and anything else my father would grow. How do I remember the varieties he grew so many years ago? I think it is because we were so dependent on what came out of the garden and his allotment that the vegetables themselves took on a standing way beyond their mundane station in my childhood. Such things as the taste of new potatoes taken fresh from the garden easily defeat the fog of memory.

My father worked on the railway as a signalman and had done so all his life having joined the Great Northern Railway in 1920, aged fourteen. When you joined the GNR you were privileged. Only the best got on the railways then and he was immensely proud of the railway all his life. Even the ravages of nationalisation and Dr Beeching when British Rail became a national joke could not dim his enthusiasm and pride in his chosen profession. He worked very hard. Our whole childhood was ruled by the rhythm of his shifts: nights, afternoons and mornings, week and week about, seven days a week. Unsuccessfully exhorted to silence on his night shift week so the poor old sod could sleep, we sometimes 'helped' in the garden on afternoon and morning shifts. When his eight-hour shift was done and he had trekked miles by bicycle from the far-flung signal boxes he worked in, he still had his garden and allotment to see to and it seems to me in retrospect that almost his whole life was spent labouring either on the railway, in the gardens or as a St John Ambulance Brigade volunteer first aider, which he was very good at and enjoyed.

During the war years he was in a reserved occupation on the railways, and he wasn't called up. So, in addition to everything else, he joined the Fire Wardens. There was a story often told in our house at the time of when the Germans dropped land mines and demolished the whole of the bottom half of our street. My father was on duty that night with the rest of the local Fire Wardens, standing by to repel German parachutists who were expected morbidly at any second. Quite why German parachutists would land at the bottom of our street in Balby, Doncaster, nobody seemed to know. But they were definitely coming one of these days, or so the justifiably paranoid thinking of the day went. The Balby Fire Wardens were convinced that that terrible day had come when they saw in a clear moonlit night two parachutes descending from an unseen aircraft. The men gathered their courage, clutched their pickaxe handles even tighter and got ready for the charge to defend King, country and womenfolk from the Hun hordes. When the parachutes were almost down, someone with a bit more sense than adrenalin recognised the parachutes for what they were.

'They're not men! They're bloody land mines! Run for it, lads!'

And run they did, so that when the land mines landed on the bottom row of houses, they were all safely away from the blast, but the houses were flattened. This story was told as a heroic feat of near death proportions or as a risible tale of the ineptitude of the Fire Wardens, depending on who was telling the story. Generally it was heroic if the men were telling it and foolhardy if the women. Whichever it was, it was the nearest my father got to hostilities, thank God, or perhaps I wouldn't be around to tell the tale.

Work, fire watching, St John Ambulance Brigade and subsistence gardening duties apart, he absolutely adored classical music of all kinds and somehow, among all this, he would find an hour now and then to listen to the BBC Third Programme concerts. Beethoven was his favourite. We hated it. It seemed so indecipherably boring to a child, but he insisted on trying to impart his passion for it onto us and was genuinely astounded and even hurt that we children or indeed his wife, could not see the genius and beauty in a Beethoven symphony.

Two years after I was born my father's titanic production efforts were rewarded with another son, James Michael, my younger brother and the sixth and final sibling. I loved Michael even then, though I think I bullied and bossed him right up to adolescence but only, I hope, in the way that elder brothers everywhere exercise their accidental advantage of size and age. We slept together in an old double bed for the next sixteen years, cuddling together under our mountain of greatcoats to keep warm in the winter and quarrelling as only tired children can on warm summer nights, greatcoats by then stored in the loft until the next mini ice age in November.

'Scratch me back, Mick, I've got a terrible itch just under me shoulder blade.'

'No. I'm buddy tired. I'm off to sleep.'

'Aw, go on,' viciously digging poor Mick in the ribs with an elbow.

'OW! That hurt! MAM! Our David's hitting me again!'

'Telltale! If you don't shut up I'll tell Mam you used the F word today, then see what you get!'

'Don't, Dava! All right, where's the itch?'

Known as our Mick at home so as not to confuse him with Father who was also a James, my younger brother quickly became my playmate even in young years. I remember very little of Douglas and Dorothy in those early years but Marguerite figured now and then. I suppose their seniority isolated them from my existence. Michael was the one I most clearly remember and being two years younger, he followed me round like a little puppy. Besides, when I was four, Douglas was eighteen, and was required to go and do his National Service as was the law then. The War was just over, this being 1946, but Douglas was sent to Germany as part of the occupying forces. I think now that the devastation and deprivation he witnessed must have been pretty awful, but insofar as I was aware at four, his letters home seemed quite jolly when they were read out to the assembled family. Either he was putting on a stiff upper lip so as not to upset his doting parents, or, as part of the victorious occupying forces he felt good about being there. The point is, he disappeared out of my life at four years old and didn't really reappear, except briefly on leave from time to time, until many, many years later, when I enjoyed him immensely. Funnily enough, I do remember his brief home leaves from the Army of the Rhine quite vividly. I would be only five or six years old but he always came with what seemed to me unimaginable largesse of chocolate bars, sweets and such, literally outside my experience in 1947. It was the riches he brought that made the impression on me, not his presence. Ah, the materialism of a five-year-old!

Marguerite's four year seniority did have one advantage to us young ones. It allowed her to get into the Saturday Afternoon Children's Matinee at Balby Cinema, and she could occasionally be persuaded to take me.

'While you're at it, take this little bugger with you. He's been a right little sod all morning. I want to get summat done this afternoon.'

'Aw Mam! He's a right nuisance when he gets there. He always wants a pee just when the film is coming on. An' my friends won't sit wi' me wi' 'im around.'

'You either take him or you're not going. Take it or leave it.'

'Ttt – oh all right' (with exaggerated bitter resentment), 'come on then, Dava, get your coat on and go and have a big pee NOW!'

Balby Cinema was a great old institution. It was owned and run by Mr Dobny who delivered the Saturday Kids Matinee as a sort of social service to the neighbourhood. Boys had to line up one side, girls on the other, unless you had a small sibling with you of the opposite sex when they stayed with their elder regardless. Girls went in first because old Mr Dobny had Edwardian manners, which was another great advantage of going with Marguerite; a coveted front row seat could be had!

As you filed in past the ticket kiosk, Mr Dobny inspected all held-out hands for cleanliness.

'You can't come in with hands like that. Why didn't you wash them before you came?'

'Me Mam's got no soap, Mr Dobny, we've got no coupons left.'

'Take this and wash your hands, then come back and show me.'

Old Dobny had a little store of soap slivers in a box for just such eventualities, shaved from a big lump of loose soap down at the Co-op likely as not.

Once inside, absolute chaos reigned. Shouting, laughing and acrobatic kids clambered over seats, fought for the best ones and generally made the noise of excitement. Eventually, old Dobny would appear on stage with a large hand bell that he would ring so loudly that your ears rang too and the mayhem was lost to the noise of the bell.

'All quieten down now!' he would roar. 'The films won't begin until there's quiet!'

And so, of course, there was quiet because the Flash Gordon cliff-hanger and the Hop-along Cassidy Western main feature were highly prized in those innocent times.

Occasionally furore would erupt in the middle of the film. The projector was turned off, the hand bell would be re-energised and dark threats of eviction made until peace was restored.

He was a good man, old Dobny, but his small cinema was already an institution out of its time and it didn't last long after that.

When I was four I went to school, which was a big, old, austere looking place with Infant and Junior buildings beside one another, just across the road from where we lived. It was surrounded by potholed tarmac playgrounds and they in turn were totally enclosed by iron railings. How these had survived the insatiable appetite for steel in the war years I don't know. Michael was upset at losing his playmate and desperately anxious to rejoin him in school as quickly as possible. So he would appear face pressed up to the railings at playtime, and once managed to break into the playground through the railings and eventually made it all the way to my classroom window, snotty nose pressed to the glass to see in the better. He had searched many windows until he found me, leaving his snotty deposit on each and causing quite a furore. Mrs Hill, my teacher, asked us all if we knew who the waif was. I had to tell her much to my shame and embarrassment at the time that he was my little brother and I was dispatched to take him home. I remember he cried when I had to leave him there to go back to school. The irony was that when he finally made it into school to join his brother, he was in a class two years behind me and the way children operate in school this was an unbridgeable chasm. Poor old Michael, but of course, he made his own society and was fine as far as I know.

Mrs Hill, my first teacher, was an absolute delight. Tall and thin with spectacles she was the essence of kindness, gentleness and care in handling four-year-olds, one of those vocational teachers who used to man schools in those days. If she hadn't been an infant school teacher it would have been a sin against children and heaven. Those few years passed easily and, I suppose, productively. I only remember isolated events from those early primary years.

I remember the family of ruffians who lived round the corner on the way to the shops; bullyboys and ne'er-do-wells the lot of them, who terrorised the other children with their ferocity and willingness to fight and brawl. I don't recall how many there were or even their name, but there were about five ranging in age from around my age up to mid teens. I lived in dread of encounters with them but fortunately they rarely came into our territory, probably having been warned off by the even more ferocious of the parents on our street.

I was sent to the Co-operative Society shop by my mother to buy some grocery or other and I had to pass the ruffians' house. I didn't mind going to the Co-op. It was a wonderful place with a wire strung cash delivery contraption overhead that took our money from the counter and delivered it to the cashier who sat in a central polished mahogany dock as if she were a miscreant in a criminal court. She received our payment from the counter hand and dispatched a receipt and change back to him with the magic Co-op number on it, 5026, to prove to your Mam that her payment had gone to swell her 'Divi', eagerly awaited once a year. The Co-op was a mutual company then and wholly owned by its members, the realisation of an early socialist dream in Rochdale, Lancashire. Each year the profits were distributed as a dividend (or divi as it was universally known) to its members, of which my mother and father were two, because they were good and committed socialists. But it was distributed according to how much you had spent in the various Co-ops during the year, so quoting your membership number on every purchase was an early and draconian discipline drilled into all of us.

There, butter was hewn from a great block on a marble top and if you were lucky the man would give you a broken biscuit from the biscuit barrel. Next to the Co-op grocery store there was the Co-op butcher and the cash conveyor went through a hole, high in the wall, from the cashier in the grocery shop to the butcher. How I marvelled at the engineering ingenuity of that contraption. I never tired of watching our cash disappearing off with a whoosh from the counter where we had just tendered it and ending up unerringly at the cashier's dock. It never dawned on me to wonder why it was necessary at all, its mere marvellous being enough to justify its existence to me. I suppose it was because they didn't trust the counter hands with the cash or maybe it was just because the Co-op in those days was the big innovator in retailing and they did it because it was the latest retail technology. In any event the same trick was repeated in the 'Big Co-op' in town, that wonderful art nouveau building in the centre of Doncaster, but the system there was pneumatic with little gondolas of our cash being amazingly dispensed vast distances about the store unseen in a maze of tubes. You couldn't even see the cashier in the big store, which made the engineering feat all the greater to me. Much to my regret, we rarely went to the 'Big Co-op' – once a year maybe at divi time when bigger purchases could be made from the annual proceeds of Co-op number 5026.

The ruffian family were out in force on what was after all their territory. Oh dread! Smelling my fear like wild dogs, they refused to let me pass unless I gave them my money as tribute. I couldn't give them Mam's precious housekeeping money clasped in my profusely sweating palm. Besides which, if I did give them it, there would be no point in proceeding to the Co-op. After considering all this and the threats of terrible physical violence that were promised by the ruffians if I didn't comply, I made an ignominious retreat and ran away home crying to my mother who, I recall, was totally unsympathetic.

Next day at school playtime I saw the youngest of the ruffian's brood down on his hands and knees playing the current version of marbles, glazed clay things because glass ones couldn't be had in those post war years, though occasionally one would be won and was highly coveted. The game involved trying to get the marble into a scooped hollow in the ground from a distance, and it took a lot of concentration. His back was to me and he was engrossed. I seized my chance. I ran up and flung my tightly balled fist round his head as hard as I could into his mouth. One tooth and a lot of blood erupted from his mouth and furore ensued. I was interrogated by the senior Infants teacher but I withheld the most shameful of my motives which was retaliation for the previous evening's defeat. I was told that my crime was so serious that, even though I was still in the Infants, I would have to appear before the Junior School Head, Mr Elliot. Oh, the terror I felt for Mr Elliot! He was, after all, the Head of the Junior School where kids got caned for their misdemeanours. As I walked nervously, no, terrified, to Mr Elliot's room I was remembering stories my elder brother Doug had told us young ones about Mr Elliot's whimsical use of Shakespeare's *Merchant of Venice* while he caned you.

'The quality of mercy is not strain'd'
WHACK!
'It droppeth as the gentle rain from heaven'
WHACK!
'Upon the place beneath:'
WHACK!
'It is twice blest;
It blesseth him that gives'
WHACK!
'and him that takes:'
WHACK
' 'Tis mightiest in the mightiest:'
WHACK

Six of the best being the common sentence, most people didn't know any more of Portia's speech but I must have fallen to wondering whether I would get into 'it becomes the throned monarch better than his crown;' or maybe even 'His sceptre shows the force of temporal power,' territory which Douglas had narrated. Mr Elliot's sceptre must certainly be about to show his force of temporal power for my terrible crime.

I remember standing in front of him in his study and his stern and implacable manner. I was shaking with fear and I involuntarily wet myself. In no time at all I had blurted out the full story as to what had motivated my heinous attack including the detailed events of the previous evening. I don't think Mr Elliot even bothered to check my story. He certainly would know the family of ruffians having endured the elder ones through his school already, and he had almost certainly administered his right of corporal punishment and invoked Portia over several of their backsides in the last few years. He must have detected a ring of truth in what I had told him, and though he could not condone what I had done, he probably thought it summary justice much in the same way as some of his own corporal punishments. I was given the sternest of stern lectures with deeply ironic threats of future serious violence to my backside if I ever hit anyone again, then made to promise that I would indeed never again lay hands on anyone. I promised with shaking voice. I would have promised to go and put my hand into the fire to get out of there. So far as I remember, news of this shameful episode never reached home or there would have been further repercussions, and the family of ruffians never bothered me again. Respect, as they say nowadays. Respect.

And then there was the winter of 1947. How could I not remember that? It was a terrible winter; icy, viciously cold and with snow, lots and lots of it. All of this was made worse by the post-war shortage of coal and fuel and even electricity. I have read since that the Attlee Government of the day were exporting coal as fast as it could be mined so as to rescue the British economy from bankruptcy caused by the War and their more grandiose plans. If this is true then damn them! They probably killed thousands of their own country-men by cold and made the already miserable existence of post-war Britain almost intolerable for the rest of us. I remember power cuts and having no fire, I remember cold chill to the bone. I remember my mother and my two older sisters going to the coalmine slag heaps where the spoil from the mines was tipped in mountainous ranges for future generations to deal with and to be killed by in Aberfan in 1966. There they could glean small pieces of coal from the slag that had managed to pass the screens and with a full day's gleaning by three of them we could have a fire that evening. Even at five years old I remember the shame and deprivation of it all and the talk in the house about picking the slag heaps being illegal. Apparently somewhere in the country, some poor wretch had been prosecuted for the theft of such hard-got coal and it was widely publicised in the newspaper, probably at the behest of the newly appointed National Coal Board, one of the first bastard children of that Attlee government.

But I also remember the drama and beauty of that terrible winter. Walking down the pavement in a canyon cut through the snow by each householder, a canyon with snow walls much higher than me and all the houses with gigantic icicles hanging from their roofs from periodic partial thaws. I remember the talk in our house about people being killed by the falling icicles which was reported in the *Daily Herald* so that we should all feel lucky to be alive in such miserable conditions. After hearing this, I scurried as fast as possible under the eaves of the house whenever I had to enter or exit lest I be skewered like a specimen butterfly by a falling icicle longer than me.

But the winter passed as all things do and it probably left me harder, tougher and yet still more resistant to colds and flu. It was only in later years that I discovered that my father had never missed a shift in that terrible winter and that despite snowdrifts as deep as houses, he still managed to bicycle his way miles every day to the signal box he was working in at the time. Indeed he was celebrated much later in life for never having missed a shift except (grudgingly) for his burst ulcer which nearly killed him and kept him in hospital for some weeks while they took away half his stomach. He truly had a fundamentalist Protestant work ethic of heroic proportions. My God, they were hard and dutiful men, his generation. They lived through two World Wars, the General Strike of 1926, and the Great Depression of the 1930s, not to mention dreadful pay and onerous working conditions and the constant fear of illness without a National Health Service. In all of that they endured humiliations and hardships beyond our comprehension in today's society. My father told me that in the General Strike of 1926, the railwaymen under the leadership of their union the NUR were first to cave in to the employers and he had to return to work before all the other unions. He was sent to work the signal box in Denaby, one of South Yorkshire's many mining towns. The miners who were predictably still on strike lined the streets and spat on him and called him scab as he passed. And still he endured. It is well that at least some celebrate them. I wish someone would do a really good job of it as Tom Brokaw did for that generation of Americans in his book *The Greatest Generation* – but then, patriotism and pride in nation is still allowed, even encouraged, in America.

Then excitement! We were moving. As people who looked after their house and were generally 'respectable', which meant we were, God forbid, never in arrears with the rent (the Council said as much in their letter to Mam and Dad. They were very proud) we were to be re-housed in a new house just built in Wheatley Hills, the posh end of Doncaster (not the poshest, that was Bessacar but that was all 'privately owned' and hopelessly beyond our ambitions). And, only the best council tenants from all over Doncaster were going! Oh, how my mother's delusions of grandeur seemed suddenly justified. Not only was it in Wheatley Hills but the new house was a semi, they said. It had gas! A gas oven with a toasting grill! Three good bedrooms! A bathroom with a toilet upstairs! A bloody dining room as well as a front room, later to be grandly referred to as 'the lounge' (Annie, my wife, is still trying to wean me from 'lounge' to 'sitting room') and a kitchen! And nobody has ever lived there before! And the houses are built round a play area for these little buggers! (pointing to me and little Michael, caught up reluctantly in the excitement). These things were said over and over again, first quietly with reverence, in case it wasn't true, and then loudly with the exuberance that such a thing demanded.

At seven years old all this meant little to me. I was perfectly happy and comfortable in Balby. I was hardened to cold and thought nothing of it any more. In any case, it was always followed by hot summer. I can still remember the delicious taste of freedom and sunshine as I bowled an old car tyre down our street having been newly released from school at the Easter holiday. Summers were also blessed with horse-drawn ice cream carts, manned by the Italian immigrant who made the ice cream in our town. He would stop in the middle of our street and those lucky enough to have the money would purchase their cone and savour it loudly with long lingering licks, generally watched by us envious ice cream paupers, begging a lick. Even though we rarely shared the delights directly, we took our pleasure vicariously, smelling and looking at the wondrous cones the lucky few had and standing at the cart counter taking it all in. I remember that the whole cart smelled of horse, not a bad smell, a mixture of horse manure, horse liniment and bran with which the beast was fed via a nosebag to keep him placid. I cannot have an ice cream to this day without an involuntary recollection of that smell. Horse crap? – ice cream. Ice cream? – horse crap, that's the way it works. And the whole contraption had the added benefit of providing horse manure for my father's garden. Whenever the ice cream cart came, Michael and I were despatched with bucket and coal shovel to trail in the cart's wake and collect the horse droppings. 'Great for the rhubarb,' said Dad. And it was.

No, I was very happy with life in our street. I loved the black-lead range in our house and the wonderful things that came out of it – cheap cuts of brisket roast beef with the most delicious dripping anyone ever tasted on a bath night in front of its fire, home made bread and its smell, warm house bricks and pyjamas in winter, and even the ruffians round the corner seemed insignificant now.

I loved the back garden, now partly lawned and flower bedecked, where I would crawl between the Jerusalem artichokes and the fence at dusk on warm summer nights to hide from the inevitable bedtime call.

I loved the streets and the woods on Western Avenue where sometimes lunatics from St Catherine's asylum would roam about ranting and raving to the wind. I'm sure they weren't dangerous, they were almost certainly shell shocked heroes from the war, but they provided a welcome diversion for us children, for there is nothing as innocently cruel as a child.

I loved my own circle of equally ragamuffin friends who played out on the street at night, hanging ropes from lamp posts to swing from, playing the season's game, hopscotch, whipping tops and the like. Making winter warmers in winter, perforated tin cans filled with burning embers and suspended on a loop of wire so you could swing it round and make the coals glow. What is it about fire that it fascinates children so?

And mud pies. I received the only terrible spanking from my father I ever had in my life as a result of mud pies. He was on night shift and trying to get some rest in bed in the afternoon. I carelessly delivered a mud pie at high velocity into the eye of one of my little ragamuffin friends, as you do, or certainly as you did in those days. Her name was Sheila. Sheila, of course, ran home crying to her mother who delivered the complainant, mud still dripping from her eyes, to our front door where she banged very loudly and indignantly, ''Ee could have taken 'er eye out!' The furore woke my dad prematurely from his night-shift induced sleep, never a wise thing to do with my father. Sheila's mother made her by now hysterical complaint to my sleep dishevelled father, bare feet, railway issue trousers not quite containing his collarless and half buttoned shirt and braces thrust over this mess as he stamped down the carpetless stairs. The undisturbed evidence of my guilt still dripped from the outraged Sheila on to the carefully washed and yellow stoned doorstep. Without a word, my father frogmarched his miscreant son to the front door from the living room where he had been sheltering from the mayhem and soundly thrashed his backside with his hand in front of Sheila's mam to give the complainant her satisfaction. Sheila's mother was eventually embarrassed by the ongoing onslaught on my backside, which was the real point of the exercise. 'Nay, Mr Fanthorpe, enough, enough,' she said. Father said he hoped she was satisfied and closed the door firmly in her face, released his pain-dancing son and without another word banged loudly back up to bed. I remember I had to sit on the cold linoleum for an hour to ease the burning of my ravaged bum while my screams subsided to wracking sobs then sultry silence as I planned darkest revenge on my father and on Sheila. It brought home to me one of the greatest of the respectable household's rules – never bring trouble to the door. Today's 'Elf and Safety culture would be appalled at our enjoyments – and their consequences.

But the neighbours weren't so bad. Sure, there was a family down the street whose name could only be whispered in our house because they had been to prison. And mixed in with the hard working families we had our small but disproportionately noisy leavening of drunks, layabouts, thieves and vagabonds who made up a society like our street, but to us kids they were the seasoning in our neighbour-hood pie.

Then there was the old man next door who insisted on carelessly killing his chickens for the pot by smashing their heads against the wall in full and appreciative view of us kids. We saw nothing particularly wrong with this especially as he then let the chickens run

about dead, with their bloodied and pulped heads dangling somewhere on their breasts and their life's blood showering everywhere.
Meat and drink to kids untutored in the finer refinements of gentle
living despite my mother's best efforts. But my mother didn't share
our enthusiasm and she hated it all with a disdain that would have
become a Duchess. Her disdain was shared for most on our street but
it turned into a violent tirade for the old neighbour and she flew at
him in a rage when she discovered his brutal abattoirial habits in front
of us young kids. He, of course, took no notice whatsoever. I don't
think he even understood why she was so outraged at what he had
allowed the children to see.

This was my world then, and we all made the best of it. To me at
the time, the best we knew was pretty damned good.

CHAPTER 2

Kathleen and James and the Broad Church

Don't hold your parents up to contempt. After all, you are their
son, and it is just possible that you may take after them.

Evelyn Waugh

NOW IS AS A GOOD A TIME AS ANY to tell you something about
my parents, Kathleen and James Fanthorpe, and the family
society I grew up in.

Kathleen, my mother, was born in 1908 in Coopers Street,
Doncaster to George and Annie Umpleby. Coopers Street was lined
on either side by three up, two down terraced houses until it petered
out into what passed for countryside in industrial Doncaster. The
further up the street you lived, the higher you ranked in the local
pecking order. My mother was born at number 48 of a hundred or
so houses, so it was 'respectable'. At the very bottom lived the Italian
immigrants, they of horse-perfumed ice cream fame. What Italian
immigrants were doing in Doncaster in the early nineteen hundreds
I never knew. In those days most people were born, worked and died
in the same town and people who chose to live or work in a place
other than their birthplace were regarded as at best eccentric and at
worst escapees from a scandalous past or the tally man. Nevertheless
here they were. It took many years of hard work, but they eventually
became a very big company and achieved international recognition
in show-jumping. Nice to think that they made it all the way from
the bottom of Coopers Street to national commercial and international show-jumping fame all founded on horse crap smelling ice
cream. Good for them!

My mother told me that when she was a flighty young woman,
the Italian family sons would walk up Coopers Street to get to the
main road and so passed her house. They were very handsome and
exotically Mediterranean and my mother quite fancied one of them.
Her interest and attraction for the exotic and different was later passed
on to my sisters who, free of Edwardian strictures by then, promptly

19

acted on it. But my mother's interest was noted by the ferocious Annie, her mother, who forbade her to even speak to them with the time of day. Such were the prejudices of the day. But for those prejudices I might have been a dark, handsome Italian!

Umpleby is a Lancashire name which made it almost as unusual as the Italians' in Yorkshire at that time. Lancashire was thought of much in the same terms as any other foreign land and worse than some to many Yorkshire xenophobes. Inter-county migration and mobility in general were quite rare back then, so much so that George's forbear, having emigrated from Manchester some many years before, was still known throughout Doncaster as Manchester Jack.

My mother had but one sister, Rhoda. Rhoda was struck down by diphtheria as a child and though she survived, it left her with a severe speech impediment, a terrible stutter, for the rest of her long life, from the damage to her larynx. Because of her near death sickness and the subsequent damage, Rhoda was always the favoured one in the Umpleby household, being let to get away with most things that my mother wasn't allowed. My mother tells a story about when they were young and mischievous girls. One Sunday after George, their father, had been to the Fitzwilliam Arms for his pre-lunch drink, he settled, replete, into an armchair by the fire and slept as was his custom. The girls took advantage of his beer- and lunch-induced stupor and cut off one half of his magnificent moustache, just for devilment. Such was the quality of John Smith's Ales in those days that George never stirred. When he woke up for Sunday tea (bread and butter with tinned peaches covered in Carnation evaporated milk, likely as not) it didn't take long for him or Ferocious Annie, his wife, to spot his lopsided loss. Kathleen took the full brunt of the fury that ensued while Rhoda was forgiven instantly and took her punishment only vicariously through my mother. This always irked my mother long into adulthood, which is some measure of how good she was in carrying a grudge.

But the moustache escapade and its consequences weren't her only grudge. She said that whenever she came in from school, a bowl of bread ingredients was always waiting for her to mix and then knead into a rising dough. Apparently, the secret of success with bread was all in the hard work of kneading which was long and tiring for a young girl, or so my mother said. Rhoda, on the other hand, was forgiven all household duties while Mother did the 'skivvying'. But if my mother begrudged the disparity in childhood treatment, it didn't stop her liking Rhoda and mostly they got on well throughout my early years.

George Umpleby, my mother's father, was a lovely man, laid-back and sociable and widely liked, despite his Lancashire roots in a foreign land. He was a handsome man, tallish and, as was the custom then, you never saw him without his three-piece suit, collar and stud, tie, silver fob watch and chain dangling over his tummy. He worked in the railway wagon works as a machinist six days a week, so on Sunday he would take immense pleasure from the Sunday lunchtime sessions in the Fitzwilliam Arms which closed at 2.00 p.m. on Sunday. Lunch was therefore served up at 2 o'clock by the diminutive but ferocious Annie but George rarely made it home before 3 p.m. This would result in a terrible scolding from the sharp tongued Annie and his excuse was always the same: 'Ah lit on so-and-so and got talking. Ah couldn't get away from him, talks the hind leg off a donkey.' Truth was, after a few pints the sociable George would need prising away from good company and he wasn't short of a few words himself. Besides which, the Fitzwilliam Arms was known to entertain lock-ins from time to time even though the licensing laws were very strict then, especially on Sundays.

Annie Umpleby was born a Widdowson in 1875. She had worked 'in service' to the Earl of Scarborough as a humble housemaid until she married George in 1903. Small and given to plumpness, she had a ferocious temper and a vicious tongue, but she was well known for the sudden switch in mood from temper to sweetness and light, so after a while everyone just waited for the storm to subside and for her sunny disposition to reappear and her scolding became less effective because of it. Sadly, she developed sugar diabetes and because the management of diabetes was only in its infancy, she died after an operation at the relatively young age of seventy-one when I was only four years old.

After that, old George used to come to our house for Mam's Sunday lunch, and every third Sunday my Dad would join him for the lunchtime session of pints and chat. He managed this because he and his fellow shift workers did twelve-hour shifts on Sundays two weeks out of three, leaving them with a Sunday break every third week. After winter lunches (or dinners as they were known in those parts), chairs and settee would be pulled round the fire and everyone settled in for a spot of keeping warm and getting up to date with family matters, ours and any others that were interesting at the time:

'Ah see that bugger down the street is back in clink ag'in.'

'Aye, six months they reckon. Ah telled thee it w'unt be long before 'e were back in.'

Old George smoked a pipe. His tobacco of choice was Battleaxe which came in a compressed block and had to be shaved off with an ancient penknife, cutting edge worn to a curve by years of tobacco block shaving. While the gossip progressed, George would be going through the post lunch ritual of tobacco shaving, rubbing up and carefully filling his pipe. Eventually, he would light his pipe and clouds of thick, acrid blue smoke would fill the room. The tobacco was so strong George would have to spit now and again to clear out the foul taste of tobacco juice. He was quite expert at this and his unerring aim would land the stream of tobacco juice sizzling on the bars of the fire from all of six feet away if necessary. We boys had immense admiration for this but needless to say, Mam was not the least bit pleased about this behaviour, but had given up trying to train her Dad out of it. She didn't have her mother's vicious disposition and tongue and had learned years before that gentle protest rolled off the laid-back George like water off a duck's back – 'Nay Kath, would tha' deny a working man 'is few pleasures?' – and no she would not, for she was very fond of her old father.

The gossip continued.

There was politics –

'Did tha read Bevan's speech in Manchester last week? 'E didn't half give the bloody Tories some stick. Vermin, he called 'em!'

'Not enough stick if you ask me,' said Mam.

And scandal –

' 'As that lass four doors away 'ad her baby yet? Maybe we'll see who the father is then.'

'Nay, ah doubt that. Little feet make big buggers run. 'E's a long way from 'ere by now.'

' 'Er poor mother, she's so ashamed, tha ne'er sees her outdoors these days.'

'Poor lass,' said Mam, who always had a soft spot for the disadvantaged, the downtrodden and the ostracised, the root of her passionate socialism. The lass in question certainly qualified for Mam's sympathy in those days, being about eight months 'in trouble' as it was euphemistically described then.

'Careful what you're saying, Dad, there's young ears about,' casting meaningful looks at Mick and me.

And family –

' 'As tha seen owt of Rhoda this week, Kath? Only she weren't too well, and that bugger Ted spending all his time Jehovah's Witnessing. How Rhoda 'ad all them kids ah don't know. You w'unt a thought Ted had found the time what with all that Jehovahring.'

'It's that stutter, George, by the time she says "No" it's too bloody late!'

'Na then, Jim, tha' shouldn't mock her affliction. She's enough to cope with as it is.'

'Sorry, George.'

And, of course, sport –

'Ah see Rovers got beat ag'in yesterday, an' they missed a penalty. 20 pounds! Ah wouldn't pay 'em in washers!'

George and my Dad had a special interest in Doncaster Rovers. In retirement George worked the turnstiles for them, when I could get in free, courtesy of Granddad George. His silver fob watch chain was hung over its full length by medals commemorating successful football campaigns he had played in as a youth, though which team he played for I never knew. I liked to believe it was Doncaster Rovers, my sporting heroes of the day, and who is to say it wasn't? At the same time Dad worked the dugouts as a St John Ambulance volunteer whenever shifts allowed. And so the conversations would go on with Michael and me sat on the floor in front of the family legs, our backs protected by them and our fronts as warm, almost literally, as toast.

Old George eventually died of bowel cancer, aged eighty-two, at our house in 1955. He had gone to the doctors with his symptoms some months before, where the doctor, among other things, tried to persuade him to give up smoking. Mam, who had gone with him, was outraged. 'Fancy telling an old man of eighty-two to give up his only pleasure in life!' she said, and defiantly kept him supplied with his Battleaxe right up to the end. George had lived independently up to this, but Mam brought him home to die where she could nurse him. A bed was brought downstairs and the lounge converted to a sickroom. It was a long and painful death. Pain management wasn't effective in those days and poor old George eventually lapsed into blessed delirium where at least he wasn't aware of the pain, though he emerged from it from time to time to rant and rave about time and events past. Michael and I were protected from all this as best as Mam could manage, but George's demise still left a lasting impression on me. I loved old George.

James, my father, was born in 1906 in Lincolnshire, where the surname comes from, and christened James Barnot Fanthorpe, the Barnot after his grandfather, I think. He was well into middle age before he discovered that his grandfather was in fact his step-grandfather. Apparently my great-grandmother had married a Fanthorpe, who promptly died on her after the birth of my paternal grandfather. In those days in rural Lincolnshire this left her in extreme trouble, there being no welfare state and only the workhouse as an alternative. However, at the funeral of her husband, she chanced to meet a distant cousin (I do hope it was a 'kissing cousin', though if not, it might explain some of the wilder eccentricities in my family) also called Fanthorpe, and they eventually married so she and my grandfather were saved to go on to greater progeny, and she didn't even have to change her name. But for that chance meeting I might not be here.

My father did well in the country school he attended and so on leaving at fourteen he was able to join the Great Northern Railway as a telegraph lad, operating the telegraph between signal boxes for the signalman. This was an apprenticeship in becoming a fully fledged signalman which he eventually achieved. He stayed a signalman for the rest of his working life, and damned proud of it, until he was sixty-seven. When he was young he worked the GNR (later LNER) east coast main line from London King's Cross to York, so he travelled a lot and lived much of the time in lodgings up and down the main line. He was very good at his job, extremely fastidious and never let his employers down. He truly knew responsibility in all its demands.

He was extremely intelligent and it was only much later in life that I discovered his immense frustration at the lack of an education to match his great intellect. As a result he had great reverence for university education and he was immensely proud when I eventually made it to university, the first and only one of his brood to manage the feat, even though it was almost an accident that I got there at all.

He did his best to assuage his own hunger for learning all his life, though I didn't recognise this until I was in my twenties. As Mark Twain said, 'When I was 16 I thought my father quite stupid. It was amazing how much he'd learnt by the time I was 21.'

He did his unconscious best to exercise his wasted intellect whenever he could. There was his classical music and composers about which he was very knowledgeable. He read widely. I remember he had a very old copy of *Paradise Lost* which he always thought valuable. It wasn't, of course, any more than any other old book, but books were always treated with reverence in our house anyway. He read *Paradise Lost* and was genuinely astounded by its scholarship. He insisted on reading passages aloud that had particularly impressed or moved him. Years later I tried to read it. I found it stultifyingly boring and almost unintelligible in places but by then my head was filled with mathematics, science and engineering and there wasn't much room for anything else for a while.

One year he invested his entire holiday entitlement by going to Summer School at Ruskin College, Oxford sponsored by his union, the NUR, where he was Branch Secretary for some years. But sadly, I think, this brief visit to his Elysian fields only served to show him how much was missing from his life, so he tried to make up for it in any way possible. There were the evangelists, Jehovah's Witnesses, Mormons and the like for example. The door knocker was regularly assailed by one or the other, the Jehovah's Witnesses generally older, earnest, direct and somewhat poor, the Mormons bright, very smart be-suited young men who sold their brand as cleverly as advertising executives selling soap powder. They were never turned away by my father because here was a source of intellectual debate. Though they never budged him from his fundamental Protestantism, he loved to debate with them about the meaning of life, God and the various, but apparently scrupulously dogmatic ways of serving Him. We all thought him quite mad to do this. The rest of us would do anything to get rid of them if Father wasn't at home. Uncle Ted, Rhoda's husband, was a passionate Jehovah's Witness and he never gave up trying to bring his version of God to our lives and hearts, even though when we saw him appear at the front gate on his bicycle we would rush to the dustbin and retrieve all alcoholic drink bottles, cigarette packets and any other detritus of a Jehovahless society to scatter carelessly around the sitting room so that he might see the hopelessness of his task. He never did though. He remained a Witness all his life and even in his nineties he was still cycling round Doncaster knocking on doors and berating reluctant listeners with Jehovah's message. Many years later my wife and I moved into a new house in Kirk Sandal, Doncaster and one Sunday morning there came a knock on the door. I opened the door and to the surprise of both of us I was face to face with Uncle Ted, bicycle clips sealing off the bottom of his trousers and *Watchtower* in hand.

'Well, I'll be blowed, it's Uncle Ted! How are you?' I said.

'It's David, isn't it, Kathy and Jim's boy? I didn't know you lived out here. I'm very well, thank you. Now about Jehovah . . .'

That was it and he was off on his much practised and largely despised message. My mother told me that Uncle Ted 'had been a right bugger' with women and drink until he was twenty-seven when he was converted to the Jehovah's Witnesses, whereupon he assumed the mantle of saintly evangelist for the rest of his long life, and regularly berated even his own family with the tenets of his new found faith: 'Enjoy this Christmas/Easter/holiday, it'll be your last. Armageddon is nigh!' was one of his favourite admonishments. There are none so righteous as the converted. Despite living well into his nineties, he never once faltered in his firm belief that this was the end of time and Armageddon was certain within the year. I don't know how many years it would have taken for him to decide that the calculations were wrong and that the end of time was a little over-rated in his faith, but seventy years of practice and annual disappointment weren't nearly enough.

His faith had inconvenient if not darker consequences for his family. Every event was to be celebrated as the last, because of the highly impending Armageddon, which must have been tiresome at the very least. Red meat was only rarely eaten and then only after full and ritualistic draining of blood. Even then, Ted wouldn't eat it and noisily resented the rest of his family enjoying it. If any of them had ever required a blood transfusion they would surely have died by his denial of it. His eldest son Les also ended up in jail because of it, having refused his conscription into the army for National Service at the command of his pacifist father Ted. Ted and Rhoda lived in Warren Close, Intake, and the house and garden where they lived were neglected and grown wild, because, I supposed, he didn't see much point in doing the garden or decorating or even keeping things tidy if the world was going to end certainly within the year if not the month, week, day or hour, such was his conviction, though my mother would have had the place spick and span even if she knew for a fact the end of the world was half an hour away.

'Warren Close? More like Rabbit Warren Close what with all them bloody kids and the long grass.'

What effect this all had on small impressionable children brought up from the cradle with the absolute belief that their time on earth was limited to a one year horizon at best, I never knew.

'Enjoy this birthday, lad, it's your last! Armageddon is nigh!'

But children are amazingly resilient and certainly there was no outward sign of melancholy or distress in my cousins, but underneath . . .? Sometimes religion has a lot to answer for.

The Mormons were different: just as fervent and with, for most people, a weird doctrine and even more unlikely roots than the Jehovah Witnesses. But they were all college educated which made their adherence to their strange and unlikely message all the more mystifying to me, and they were skilled in debate and proselytising, which is why my father gave them his time. They were capable of taking the mickey out of themselves though, as part of their armament in gaining their subject's confidence. Many years later, I worked for an American chief executive who was a very senior Mormon in his Tabernacle. He told a story over dinner one night of how he had got his very first job in sales. He had just done his required Mormon two years of door knocking Mormon evangelism and was then allowed, even encouraged, by his Church to go into gainful employment since they would gain ten per cent of his earnings, the tithe still being in place in that Church. He was interviewed for a salesman post and the interviewer asked him what he'd been doing for two years since leaving college. The Chief explained that he had been evangelising his Mormon faith door to door. The interviewer asked him what his message had been, and, needing no second invitation, the Chief launched into his well practised story of the Mormon Church and its unlikely roots. The interviewer thought for a few seconds then told him if he could sell that crap he could sell anything and he was hired. And so, as they say, began a great career.

All of these things kept my father from the worst of his intellectually starved frustrations, but I have often wondered what he would have achieved if he had been born fifty years later and had had the educational opportunities that chanced my way. I know he was capable of great intellectual achievement and would have been a great man to a much wider society than just me.

My parents' marriage was a strange affair. My father loved my mother dearly, I am sure, though grindingly hard work and his frustrations made him very testy and moody from time to time, so it wasn't necessarily obvious. My mother, on the other hand, professed frankly not to love him to us youngsters in our teens. When Father was on afternoon shift and out of the way, my mother would constantly berate him and complain of his bad temper and his 'symphonying'. She had her own frustrations, not least of which were the constant lack of money and the sheer drudgery of bringing six children into the world and caring for them. She had great delusions of grandeur and firmly believed she should have been a famed singer but for the burden of James Barnot and her offspring. I think the root of this bile was the death of Pauline in 1940 exacerbated by her poverty and drudgery. She did tell me a terrible story, though, of how she and Father came to be married and if it is true, it would go a long way to explain her disgust at life's treatment of her as a prisoner of circumstance.

When she was eighteen, my father, being an itinerant signalman for the GNR, frequently visited Doncaster to work its signal boxes and he needed lodgings. My grandparents, needing the extra money, let one of their rooms to lodgers and my father duly joined the Umpleby household as a lodging tenant where, of course, he met my mother. Over some time my father fell in love with my mother and courted her assiduously. But according to her, some thirty years on from the event, my mother wasn't so keen and didn't fully return his feelings for her. Her story was that things eventually came to a head when my father wrote to old George and asked him for his daughter's hand in marriage, as was the protocol then. My grandparents, George and Annie, were very keen. They liked James Barnot and thought he was a good catch for their daughter. They discussed this prospect with their daughter Kathleen who refused the proposal point blank and a terrible row ensued. But George and Annie would not relent and, according to my mother, physically forced her to write accepting my father's proposal of marriage in her own hand but against her will. George then sealed her forced acceptance in an envelope and, just to rub it in, accompanied my mother to the post box to see it, and eventually her, safely dispatched, again by her own hand. And so, according to Kathleen, she was married in 1927.

I was never sure about this story. Mam didn't tell lies, but she did have a capacity for self justifying delusion. She was quite convinced that Edward VIII didn't abdicate, but had been 'got rid of' by the 'right wing'. Edward's dalliances with Hitler and the Third Reich were ignored in order to bolster her left of Labour view of the world and of King Edward who had earned my mother's admiration because he expressed sympathy for the poor during his tours in the Depression years.

I know Victorian and Edwardian parental authority was pretty powerful and that such things as her forced marriage were possible but to go along with it through the entire engagement and wedding process always seemed a bit unlikely to me. Douglas, my eldest brother and first born, tells me that he thought they were happy in his childhood, despite the privations of the thirties, and children are usually good instinctive judges in these things. However he also related that when he was about fourteen, he thought Mother was on the verge of what would have been a disastrous affair with a local butcher, and he had to put a stop to it before Father found out. But that, of course, was in the immediate aftermath of Pauline's death and my mother was suffering under her burden of guilt and probably trying to pass some of it on to my father.

And then there were six children from this non-love match. God only knows how many she would have had if she had loved him! Whatever the veracity of her story, it was her tragedy to live most of my life at least with an increasingly corrosive bitterness which only began to fade in her later years, and even then it popped out now and again. When she was old and my father had died, she spent Christmas with us together with my wife Annie's mother for company. Annie's mother, Molly, was fiercely Roman Catholic Irish of the old school but they got on well together. On Boxing Day, Annie asked me to take them out for a run to the seaside about four miles away while she tidied up and got lunch ready. The two old matrons sat in the back of my Jaguar with me up front for all the world like the hired chauffeur. My mother doubtless felt this mode of transport was the least she deserved while Molly loved the novelty of the luxury. They fell into easy conversation as if the chauffeur didn't exist.

'To be sure you're a very lucky woman, Mrs Fanthorpe.'

She always called my mother 'Mrs Fanthorpe' even though they got on well. My mother accepted this as due deference and addressed Annie's mother as 'Molly' in return.

'To be blessed with all these lovely children,' Molly continued.

'Blessed? BLESSED? I would have done away with all of 'em if I could have, Molly!' my mother replied.

Molly was absolutely dumbfounded and genuinely shocked to the core of her Irish Catholic soul.

'No, no, Mrs Fanthorpe. You don't mean that!' shouted Molly.

'Oh aye I do!' said my mother with gusto to accentuate her strength of feeling. She, of course, did not have the benefit or the inhibitions of an Irish Catholic education.

Molly searched about for some argument to refute this. Back in her ancestral home in Ireland she would have had my mother up in front of the priest within the hour but none was to be found in the back of a Jaguar on Seaton Front on Boxing Day, and in any case Kathleen belonged to the Godless Protestants.

'What about Michael? He's done your shopping and looked after you all those years; surely you wouldn't want him . . .' Molly couldn't even finish the sentence for fear of the damage it might do to her mortal soul.

There was grudging acceptance of Michael's right to life from my mother on the basis that he had been a good and dutiful son, but as for the rest of them, well . . .

With an involuntary shudder, Molly rapidly changed the subject and we continued our tour of Hartlepool's seaside high spots, the chauffeur mildly amused at their utter detachment from him in the back seat and at Molly's stout Catholic defence of his being. He had heard it all before from his mother.

Poor old Kathleen, my mother who I loved. My heart still bleeds at the great sadness and hopelessness, the sheer bloody waste of it all. God rest her.

CHAPTER 3

Wheatley Hills – the green and pleasant land and what the Little Tykes did to it

And did those feet
In ancient times
Walk upon England's green and pleasant land?

William Blake: 'Jerusalem'

A ND SO WE MOVED FROM BALBY to the coveted Wheatley Hills. It was all we had been told, a lovely new semi on Thorne Road just east of the General Hospital and at seven, knowing no better, I thought it quite perfect. It was set back from the main road on a service road with a grassy embankment separating the two roads. It had good gardens to front, side and rear and it was, as had been predicted, part of a periphery of houses surrounding a meadow land play area for us kids. Truly a house built for heroes.

Father set to work cultivating the garden land from the builder's wilderness, an extra but unresented demand on his energy and time, and Mam set to work decorating and turning a house into a home, all novel experiences to Michael and me who had only lived in one house all our lives.

I remember the gas oven most of all, an astounding machine to us kids back then and quite the height of modern domestic sophistication to my mother. With a stretch up to the grill, I could make my own toast and without the inconvenience of burning the skin off my knuckles in front of a glowing fire. I lived on toast for a full month after we moved in, so taken was I at the novelty of it all.

'What would you like for your tea, Dava? Not bloody toast again! You'll turn into a loaf of bread if you keep this up!'

While all this was going on Michael and I set about discovering our new world. And what a green and pleasant land it was. There was the field at the back, which the Council probably intended levelling and cultivating with lawn seed so that kids could play football. Adults always thought kids wanted to play football on grass. Not so. Football was for the street in front with its hard and

31

unforgiving but true tarmac surface and where you could use the camber to your cunning advantage and the kerbs as extra wingers for 'closet door' passes. Thankfully, they never got round to it and the field remained a wilderness all my childhood.

No, what grassy areas were for was finding skylarks' nests, mice hunting, making fireplaces and frying the hated red ants on treacle tin lids, rolling about in, playing hide and seek in when the grass and weeds were high enough in summer and, of course, digging holes in to make underground dens with sod roofs. The dens also served to trap unwary strangers.

'Bloody hell! What was that I just fell in?'

'It's a bloody great hole covered in sticks and grass sods!'

'I told thee we should have walked round by the road instead of cutting through here.'

'It's those bloody Fanthorpe kids! I'll have to have a word with Jimmy. They'll break some poor sod's legs one of these days.'

'Or else their necks. The sooner the bloody Council gets summat done about this mess the better.'

But thankfully, the Council never did, not in my time anyway, and the skylarks, the field mice and ants lived on behind our house despite our best efforts for all the years of my childhood.

Then there was the Boating Lake about a mile down the road where, on the rare occasions you could prise sixpence out of your Mam or Dad, you could hire a rowing boat and splash inexpertly about for a full hour. That was time enough to land on one of the two forbidden islands, blind side of the park attendant, and search for duck eggs and moorhens' nests and build forts to repel imaginary Germans, for they were still imminent as far as we were concerned.

The periphery of the park was still relatively wild then and wooded and therefore almost as good as the lake and boats in our judgement. There you could climb to the very top of trees for a pigeon's egg and raid bushes for the small birds' nests, safe from the park keeper's admonishments because he could never see you in there. And in the shallows of the lake at the wildest end there were reed beds with frogs, toads and newts, and spawn followed by tadpoles in spring. These were carried home in a Robertson's jam jar, and fed with raw meat dangled in the water from a string while we watched the miracle of transformation from tadpole to frog – first the back legs sprout, then the front legs then the tail shed and, hey presto! – a tiny frog! The miracle never failed to amaze me spring after spring.

I got my first practical demonstration of yet more of God's miracles coming home from the boating lake one summer day. God and Jesus and the Bible stories were taken very seriously in schools back then, so we were very familiar with God's power, even though we had a healthy adult scepticism about the actual practice of those powers by God. Besides which, my father was certain He existed, believing as he did in the literal word of the Bible, Genesis and all, and that was good enough for me.

It had been very hot and a terrible thunderstorm was gathering but it was almost upon us before we noticed, so engrossed were we. What were we to do, a mile from home with torrential rain and, worse, lightning promised? We set off home at a brisk pace and I suddenly thought of a possible solution. We would pray! God must control thunderstorms, it stood to reason. I had seen pictures of Him, old and much bewhiskered AND with lightning bolts coming out of His hands. So we prayed loudly and fervently the whole mile, Michael and I, that the storm wouldn't break until we got safely indoors at home. The storm rumbled ominously in the distance and it got darker and darker but we finally made home and scrambled indoors. At the doors closing the heavens opened instantly, the lightning flashed and the thunder crashed and Michael and I wondered long after at the power of the Almighty, all scepticism banished.

If you crossed Thorne Road and went down to the edge of Intake, just by the racecourse, you also found what was to become the greatest of our childhood wildernesses – Sandal Beat Woods. A vast deciduous forest riddled with animal tracks, it extended miles, all the way to Armthorpe Pit and beyond. Here, though, it was split by the railway serving the pit, and that was a natural boundary beyond which even we intrepids wouldn't venture. Railway line and pit meant civilisation and we had a healthy wariness of civilisation when we were on adventure. Civilisation meant Park Keepers, the Bobbies, Watchmen and all other forms of authority that any sensible child bent on delicious freedom would keep as far away from as possible.

Rumour had it that this had once been the outer reaches of Robin Hood's Sherwood Forest and who knows, maybe it was. After all, Robin Hood's Well was just north of Doncaster on the Great North

Road, we had heard. In any event, the thought added an extra frisson of excitement to the place.

In the long summer holidays we would disappear off after breakfast with a bottle of water in an old lemonade bottle and a slice of bread and butter wrapped in greaseproof paper and my mother wouldn't see us until dusk, for which she was very grateful. It never occurred to anyone, let alone my mother or father, that we were in any danger from paedophiles and the like. It just wasn't like that back then. As far as Michael and I were concerned, paedophiles hadn't been invented yet, so even a notion of any such danger was missing. Mam and Dad were just glad that peace reigned in the house, Father for his sleep, and Mother just because it was a respite from the drudgery of attending to us. They had not the slightest concern at our day-long absences.

We would arrive home black bright and famished and after tea we would be packed off to bed to sleep the sleep of the just, all Germans and Sheriff's men having been vanquished during the day.

Closer to home was Flint Wood and Chat's Pond. Chat's Pond was less than a quarter of a mile away at the side of the hospital and served up sticklebacks as well as the ubiquitous frogs with their spawn. The pond was heavily polluted with discarded rubbish but we thought little of this. It was water and mud and reed beds and it was within easy striking distance of home when time of day or sheer exhaustion forbade a long trek to Sandal Beat Wood. What more could a boy ask for? The poor sticklebacks cared though. The pollution, while not exterminating them, nevertheless gave them awful fungal growths and lesions, which strange as it may seem, made them even more interesting to morbidly curious children.

The pond stood on the opposite side of Armthorpe Road to a great old house, then derelict and falling down, which we liked to believe had been the Chats' home at one time or another and this wreck was another target of our unwelcome attentions. This being a very old house and falling down, it was bound to be haunted and worth our wary attention for that alone. Besides, you could climb between stories and wreak all sorts of further damage without redress. Yes, Chats' and its pond were always worth a visit if you were pushed for time.

One winter's day when it was too cold to venture far, we were at the pond to slide on the ice. The ice wasn't thick enough, however, but we didn't recognise this until with a crack! – it broke and I plunged through into three feet deep icy cold water and thick, black, evil smelling mud. I had quite a struggle to get out. My chums thought this hilarious but I was as cold as I have ever been and getting colder, wet through in the frosty air. I trudged home crying, leaving black muddy footprints and a trail of water all the way from the pond to our back door where I daren't enter because of the mess I would cause. Michael ran in and got my mother.

'Whatever have you been doing, lad? You look as if you've been down the pit for a month! Ooo, the smell!'

By now I had lost all feeling from the cold and my mother took reluctant pity and stripped the filthy sodden clothes off me at the back door at stretched arm's length. It made no difference to me. My condition was the same, clothes or no clothes, all feeling in my limbs gone. I was only then allowed entry over spread newspaper and dispatched to the bath to get rid of the awful smell and mud. I cried even louder then as the hot aches took over where the cold had left off. But eventually, the hot aches went and the hot bath felt wonderful, even though the water was by now as black as I had been. At least the smell was now diluted. How strange to have a bath on a Saturday, I thought.

Even the green and pleasant land sometimes had an unfortunate side, but I still wouldn't have changed it for Balby. As the warmth soaked through I thought that Wheatley Hills was still too good to be true.

CHAPTER 4

Is this your dog, Missus?

Every dog should have a boy.

Apologies to Mark Twain (who should have said it)

WHEN I WAS ABOUT EIGHT OR NINE, my joys in the green and pleasant land were compounded and even complete. I got a dog, or rather he got me.

His mother was a pedigree golden cocker spaniel who lived, much to my previous envy, three doors away at one of our neighbours'. She was a beautiful dog, placid but boisterous with children and quite the prettiest of the spaniel breed. Her name was Noni, which, though I didn't know it then, is Italian for grandmother. How very apt this turned out to be as her offspring, my dog, proliferated all over Doncaster and probably, later knowing his vast enthusiasm for procreation, over much of the West Riding.

Noni, being a pedigreed dog, was watched over carefully when she was in season to preserve her pedigree for future breeding, but one day, while let out into the garden for the usual early morning offices, she was spotted by a wily and randy old mongrel who, not being a respecter of anyone's fences or her pedigree, promptly leaped the fences and, well, procreated with her. Too late Noni's outraged owner spotted what was going on, and though the rampant old mongrel had to flee with a bucket of cold water, a boot and a half house brick pursuing his rear end, he probably thought it well worth the penalty.

In time Noni produced a big litter of black and white puppies and since one of my chums was the son of the house, I was introduced to them. They were simply beautiful. In my young life I had never seen anything quite so beautiful and my heart was captured. Noni allowed us to handle them freely, being the placid and lovely natured dog that she was, and within days I had singled out one pup for my besotted affections, or rather he sought me out. He was the bravest and therefore the most forward of the litter and in time he would readily seek my hand to lick and eventually chew with his needle

36

sharp teeth. I harassed my reluctant parents with a pleading campaign to be allowed to have him and promised that all his needs would be attended to by me – and that they wouldn't have to do a thing – as a million or more children had done before me and have since. They weren't that difficult to persuade. They had had several dogs of their own in their married life so they were doggy people at heart. Besides, they knew the fate of the pups if owners couldn't be found. To be tied in a sack with some house bricks and thrown in the canal was the common fate of unwanted animals in those days. Eventually it was agreed and I lived in fevered anticipation for the pups to be weaned and old enough to be taken from their mother.

Patch was to be his name, not very original but very apt. Where his mother was golden from her nose to her tail and silky long haired, he was black and white in patches all over and short wire haired. His chest was wide and he was stocky with muscle, testament to the large proportion of terrier in his rascal mongrel sire. Incongruously, despite his terrier characteristics, he inherited his mother's long spaniel ears and her retriever jowls, so he looked a strange mixture of potential ferocity in his body and soppy playfulness in his head. He was perfect. The dog had found his boy and the boy was his.

There followed the rituals of mongrel puppy ownership: the first night's separation from his mother and the whimpering and crying at night as he got used to being outside of the warm snuggle of his doting mother and his siblings for the first time. Father insisted that the dog must know his place in the house so he was provided with a box in the corner of the kitchen, a position that was maintained all his life. I was not allowed to intervene in his enormous sadness in losing his mother at nights by bringing him up to my bed to comfort him.

'Nay lad, he 'as to get used to it, and if tha teks 'im up to bed we'll ne'er 'ave a bit of peace. 'E stays where 'e is.'

I didn't like it, but Dad was right and surprisingly soon, in just a few days, Patch was sleeping through the night, content in his new home. It was a tribute to my father's wisdom and forbearance that he endured the loss of his precious sleep to do the right thing.

Patch the cuddly puppy rapidly grew up to become Patch the retrieving adventurer with his boy, Patch the Lothario and Patch the scourge of all other male dogs he laid eyes on.

From his mother Noni he inherited, as well as his ears, an insatiable appetite for retrieving together with the jowls to achieve it. When, in roaming the woods, we collected the odd bird's egg, Patch would whine and whimper until I let him carry the prize home in his retriever's soft and padded mouth. Likewise the odd dead things that we thought interesting enough to take home, as boys do, he would insist on carrying them all the way home. Nothing would deny him this privilege and fulfilment of his mother's genes.

One of our favourite 'tortures' of each other was to pin the victim down and have Patch come and lick their face until they screamed for helpless mercy. Patch's enthusiasm for licking a boy's face was only exceeded by his enthusiasm to lick himself, bird's eggs and dead things so it's astounding we didn't all catch some terrible disease but we had a blind faith in a myth of the day that dog's saliva was antiseptic. But we didn't catch anything, at least as far as I know, and it only added to the great natural immunity all kids enjoyed in those days.

But from his father he inherited all the ferocity, cunning hunter/killer skills, and utter determination of the terrier his father had undoubted been several generations of randy garden trysts and buckets of cold water ago. With people, he was fine: always happy to greet them with a frantic wagging of his tail stump (abruptly docked by my father in puppyhood). He liked children even more since he instinctively recognised kindred spirits in a lust for life, play and adventure while roaming in our wilderness woods.

With other dogs, he was their worse nightmare, a nightmare shared by my poor mother when irate owners called to complain. He could not abide to be in the presence of another male dog. Because he roamed free in the world with his boy, he assumed the world to be his territory, not to be violated by any other dog. So if we came across another dog, usually around the neighbourhood, sometimes on leashes (which Patch rarely was unless pulling us on our go-cart), sometimes minding their own business, safe, so they thought, in their own front yard, his fur would go up and he would be on them with all the savagery of his rascally mongrel forebears. Size of dog didn't matter and he never had the respect for ferocity of breed recognised by humans. All they had to be was dog. Fur up, fangs bared and snarling he would have the job half done before I ever had time to drag him reluctantly off the poor victims who up until then had been strutting Alsatians, Dobermans, huskies and the like, confident in their ability to defend their territory. Not surprisingly, proud owners could be quite miffed about the bloody mess their dog had become in a matter of snarling, teeth flashing seconds, especially when, as well as the injured affection they gave their dog, the dog was also an expensive pedigree. Such encounters, and there were many, sometimes resulted in a call at our house from the outraged owner.

'Is this your dog, missus?' pointing at Patch who invariably accompanied anyone who answered the front door, smiling and wagging his stump frantically in greeting. You wouldn't think butter would melt in his mouth now. There then would follow a catalogue of Patch's crimes against his extremely valuable and well loved dog. This was invariably followed by dark threats of 'Kicks to his arse' and the one my respectable Mam feared most: 'Report to the Authorities.' My poor Mam. She would apologise profusely, promise that it would never happen again and that Patch would henceforth always be leashed until the accuser was satisfied with her contrition and her humiliation. I don't recall that my father ever answered these calls at the door, especially when he was on nightshift, or the consequences would have been much more severe, both for Patch whose manhood would have been somewhere in front of his ears after my father had finished kicking him, and for me. I think that Patch and I only got away with it because the complainants couldn't reconcile the savage, bloody damage to their dogs with this benign, diminutive, friendly dog at our doorstep, and in any case, wouldn't want to admit too widely that their Alsatian/Doberman/husky had lost in battle to this little nobody. Mother's words to me after these events were never directly severe. She was too worn out for that.

'You'll have me in St Catherine's [the then lunatic asylum] before I'm forty,' she would say with the utter resignation of the defeated. That hurt even more than harsh words but Patch still ran free.

As well as all male dogs, Patch couldn't abide cats. This wasn't based on territorial rights as with other dogs. No, this was based on a bitter lesson, one of the rites of passage for all dogdom. When he was just a pup I had him out for a walk and on our return a mangy ginger tom was skulking under our hedge. Patch saw him and thought, as he thought about almost everything then, 'What fun!' He ran up to the cat with his usual greeting of doggy smile, stump and whole rear end wagging furiously. The mangy old tom proceeded to teach him one of dog-life's oldest lessons – cats hate dogs with all the sneaky, feline cunning that is characteristic of their species. They do not wish to play with dogs. The cat reached out from under the hedge with a clawed-out paw and fetched Patch deep scratches right across his wet, black nose in one vicious swipe. With the possible exception of one other obvious part of his anatomy, the later object of many aggrieved dog owner's aim, his retriever's nose was the most sensitive place the old tom could have chosen. Its target had been chosen with the wisdom of an old street wise cat for he knew that this was about as dog-disabling as it gets. Blood flowed freely from Patch's lacerated nose, tears flooded his eyes and he howled piteously as he ran blindly back to me, the leader of his small pack. But there was nothing I could do. The wily old tom having satisfied himself that his disabling objective was achieved stalked nonchalantly away as if nothing had happened, his disdain witness to his superiority.

Never again would Patch trust a cat. Never again would he allow a cat within one hundred yards of him unless he had their backside clearly in sight and it was retreating at least as fast as he was pursuing it. Thereafter his fury with cats was at least the equal of that with other dogs and he cleared our immediate vicinity of them, regularly. Though his ferocity and size was more than a match for cats, they had the propensity of cool cunning and ready-made instincts. Patch once spied a cat in our back garden, obviously a newcomer to the neighbourhood or he would have been anywhere but in Patch's kingdom. Patch tore at the cat with all the pent up hatred that only a severely lacerated nose many years before could muster in him. The cat, surprised, took flight. Figuring that he was going to be overhauled by the furious, faster dog, the cat opted, just like any good defending fighting force, for the high ground and leapt to the top of the fencepost, about five feet high. Patch, all fifteen inches of him, tried to leap after the cat. At each futile leap, the cat raked Patch's head with the deadly claws. Such was Patch's breeding that his fury would not allow for discretion or any rational doggy thought for that matter and he persisted with his futile attempts to reach the cat until his spaniel ears were in bloody tatters and his head covered in blood. Still he couldn't see that the cat was his intellectual superior in warfare and he would surely have died fighting if I hadn't come outside to see what the furore was. The cat, recognising immediately that superiority had suddenly passed to the other side, jumped down from his post and took flight again in a mad zigzag sprint across the back field to avoid any human launched guided missiles that might follow him. That was always the difference. Cats had cunning, brains and generally knew the score. Patch, on the other hand, had terrier ferocity, blind venom and a determination without discretion that would be the end of him without his pack leader. Clearly, when it came to cats, Patch had no brains.

If cats got the better of him in tight corners, mice and rats stood no chance, and he became a renowned neighbourhood mouser and ratter. It wasn't that a mighty mouse had bit him unexpectedly as a pup and hence planted a lifelong hatred in him. This was pure terrier instincts and blind determination so there wasn't the fury in him when seeking and killing mice. That stupidity was reserved for cats. It was just what he had been pre-programmed to do and he went about it with utter detachment, efficiency and blind devotion to the task in hand. The play area at the back of our house was riddled with field mice and if Patch got the scent, he would trace it all the way back to the mouse-hole in the grassy banks and he would start digging. This was the exact replica of the cat fights. The dog was cool and remorseless. The mouse imagined he was safe, complacent two feet inside a meadow bank in his cosy nest and sat it out. Bad decision! It sometimes took Patch two hours digging to reach the nest, but reach it he would. No force on earth could stop him. If you dragged him away to go for your tea, he would return to his dig as soon as he could escape the house. If you tried to divert him with a favourite pastime, he would give the prospect a millisecond of thought and go back to his digging. No, if a mouse was smelt by Patch, it was a dead mouse walking. He once turned over a large stone being used for path hedging in Dad's vegetable garden to reveal a mouse's nest complete with sixteen mature young ones. The mice, of course, scattered in all directions radially from their nest site. They hadn't counted on a bred terrier's speed and efficiency. With a nip and a toss of his head all sixteen lay dead, probably all within less than thirty seconds and Patch stood back to receive his due acclamation as if nothing had happened, any thoughts of victorious cats dispersed from his mice-fevered brain. As a scene of miniature, efficient carnage it was unsurpassed and we were mightily impressed. Patch's street cred spread far and wide and on several occasions neighbours asked me to sort out their mice and rat problems, usually in their outhouses, there being no cats available in our neighbourhood for some inexplicable reason.

'Tha knows, I can't keep a bloody cat for no price. Three ah've had now, all of 'em gone in a week! Ah can't understand it, we feed 'em well, give 'em a basket, look after 'em rate well, but the buggers ne'er stay. One of 'em turned up t'other side of town in Balby, the other two, God only knows. There's summat they don't like round 'ere, an' that's a fact.'

That's a true fact, Patch smiled.

On the other hand, Patch also had a prodigious appetite for procreation which had serious side effects and ultimately led to his demise. When let out first thing in the morning, he wouldn't do the obvious thing. He would stop in his headlong rush for night's relief and gently savour the air, head tilted up to catch every nuance in the breeze like Hannibal Lector savouring a particular fine liver. If there was a bitch in season within five miles to windward or two miles to leeward, he would know. From that moment on, no matter what the constraint and attention, he would escape the house and pack leadership to seek her out. At the first and slightest opportunity he would hurtle, head down, full pelt, out across the garden and service road, up the embankment and, totally obsessed with his objective, straight across the A17 trunk road, oblivious to the traffic and terrible injunctions – 'Patch! PATCH! Come back here you little bugger! Damn you!' He would disappear off in this way for hours, eventually returning shamefaced and cringingly deferential, filthy from head to tip of stump, twigs and debris caught up in his ears and smelling, as he preferred, of dung and 'dog'. Near miss drivers from the trunk road, bobbies and irate pedigree bitch owners were regular complainants at the door.

'Is this your dog, Missus . . .?'

None of them could complain about Patch doing what came naturally, but they could and did complain bitterly about his apparent freedom to do so.

Father built a fence between the house side and the boundary fence that totally enclosed the back garden. No good. When at first Patch discovered he couldn't jump this, he just dug underneath using his prodigious ratting skills. This was long work though, allowing time for him to be discovered excavating his escape and restrained. So he honed his high jump skills and soon, it was as if the fences didn't exist and he ran free at will, as ever. Over time, you couldn't help but notice the proliferation of small black and white patched terrier mongrels with long ears across Wheatley Hills, Intake and for up to five miles around.

The trouble with Patch was that he was fearless. He didn't fear bigger dogs, he didn't fear cats even when he should have done and he didn't fear the retribution that he knew would inevitably follow his amorous absconding. There was only one thing that struck abject terror into him and reduced him to a quivering, whimpering wretch. It was, of course, a four letter word.

'Bath!'

I didn't do it very often because he hated it so and because practically, it was a very difficult thing to do. But sometimes when he was sprawled in front of the fire at night jerking and whimpering as he dreamt his doggy dreams of mice and rabbits and boys running through the woods, you could almost see the heat driven doggy fumes rising off him and my father would have something to say.

'David! That bloody dog smells like a polecat. I'n't it time tha give 'im a bath?'

No matter how deep Patch's sleep, no matter how sweet the dreams of mice and rabbit extermination, at that one word 'bath' he would jerk awake, look round fearfully for the imminent executioner, then slink off, quivering, to his basket in the kitchen and make himself look small.

'Ay allrate Dad,' with resignation, 'ah'll do it tomorrow.'

The next day, the campaign would be planned and the awful thing done. First you had to coax Patch to come upstairs to the bathroom without him realising the object. If he knew you wanted him up there to bath him, it would be the devil's own job to even get him there, let alone into the bath. 'Patch! Patch! Mice!' would generally do the trick. It was a mean deceit but it was better than dragging him by the collar, his legs stiff and dug in, his collar straining his neck to choking point. Once bounded upstairs, eager for mouse battle, there was nothing for it but to grab him bodily, ignoring the awful smell and its source, and carry him now struggling wildly as if for life itself, to the prepared and waiting bath. Once in the bath he went into a sort of quivering, enduring trance while the awful work was done, licking any soap that came within tongue's reach, not because he liked the taste but much in the same way he would lick any offensive substance from his pelt.

Throughout this phase of the campaign it was essential that one boy held him firmly at all times while the other did the dirty work with the soap. Otherwise, Patch would take whatever opportunity arose to leap from the bath and hurtle as fast as possible as far from it as he could get. Catching a soap-greased and anyway slimy dog intent on escape is no easy matter and it would take at least ten minutes of frantic pursuit round the house while Patch shook dirty soapsuds over all the furniture, Mam and furiously evasive sisters. No, far better to hold on to him while the terrible job was done. Once rinsed, the next trick was to get as much water as possible off him with an old towel before he realised it was over, otherwise he would shake it off with such vigour that Mick and I would be wet through and the ceiling dripping. Finally it was safe to let go and Patch would spring out of the bath and celebrate by running round the house in delirious circles until the awful memory faded and he could contemplate getting outside and rolling in the nearest pile of horse dung again. It was a thankless and ultimately pointless task bathing Patch.

I suppose in dog terms he had a long and happy life, occasional baths apart. He had a boy to enjoy for the best years of his life. He wandered with his boys for endless summer days through the woods and wild places of east Doncaster, played his games with them, carried their wild eggs and dead treasures home with them, and really, apart from them having a bath (quiver!) every Sunday, he was a boy with four legs. Either that or they were dogs with two legs.

In the end, though, the endless procession of complainants and threats of official intervention decided his fate. When I was seventeen and at work as an apprentice, Mam took him down to the RSPCA and had him put down. I was devastated and promised never to forgive her. With time, of course, I totally understood her weariness at the constant complaints and worse, the threat of legal action. He had had nine doggy years with his boy, but that was over anyway, his boy's head and time now filled with the usual adolescent obsessions and the rigours of acquiring a profession, and his life would have been empty without a companion to roam free through the forests and wild places. Perhaps it was for the best, having lost his boy, but I still think of Patch and his unreserved love. Every dog should have a boy.

CHAPTER 5

George

Over-sexed,
Over-paid
And worse,
Over here.

Tommy Trinder

G EORGE WAS A BIG, LOUD and swaggering but generally likeable
Yank. He came into our lives when I was ten, and more
importantly, Dorothy, my eldest sister, was nineteen. He was a GI in
the US Air Force based at Lindholm eleven miles east of Doncaster.
He was tall, big boned and, even then, inclined to fat but he had a
charisma that was partly due to his exotic American-ness in austere
post war Britain and partly because he exuded the natural confidence
of a regular winning brawler.

In the week he worked at the base in the motor pool as a Staff
Sergeant of the US Airforce; that is when he wasn't busted down to
Private for brawling or drinking or, usually, both. On Saturday night
though, he, together with all his compatriots, descended on Doncaster
town centre to trade their ample money for whiskey and their nylons
for favours and generally have a good time. This consisted of getting
roaring drunk and upsetting the local men by corralling all the pretty
women, which in turn led to brawls and fights that usually started in
the pubs then inevitably spilled out onto the streets. George had no
inhibitions about the vast enjoyments to be had in this activity and a
Saturday night that didn't include a bottle of Canadian Club, a pretty
girl and a good brawl was counted a failure and waste of a weekend.

He came from a small country town in hillbilly Illinois and told
stories about it and his childhood there that only added to his
all-American mystique. He told us that his grandmother was a full
blooded Cherokee who, when he told her he was to be posted to
Europe, could not comprehend what he was talking about.

'Where is Europe?' she asked.

'It's across the Atlantic Ocean, Grandma,' replied George.

'What is the Atlantic Ocean?' she persisted.

45

'It's a great sea,' said George.

'Ah, a great water; you're going to Can-a-da!' she said, understanding at last.

'No, no, Grandmother, it's much further than that and a much bigger sea.'

'There is no bigger sea than the great lakes,' she said, puzzled, but convinced her grandson was pulling her leg.

George gave up.

He told us his father had once been elected Sheriff of their small town, and while on patrol one night, down by the railroad tracks, he saw a shadowy figure dodging about between the railroad cars. He challenged the figure and ordered him to stop. The figure immediately took flight and George's father, assuming the fugitive was up to no good, loosed off a couple of shots to warn him to stop. Unfortunately, one shot hit the fleeing figure and killed him stone dead. Only then did George's father discover that the fugitive was just a railroad bum whose natural reaction to any authority, sensibly, was to put as much space as possible between it and him as quickly as possible. George's father got scared now that he might be held responsible for the death as an unjustified homicide and so bundled the body into a railroad freight car that was leaving, probably to rumble for a thousand miles before stopping, and went home. He never heard anything more about it, or so George said.

He told us about his small town birthplace and its attitudes and values. He had inherited a very strong racial prejudice from his home town, shared by many Americans and by the American forces at the time. He said there was a notice at each end of the town main street which read:

'Nigger, don't let the sun set on your head.'

He saw nothing wrong with this at all, it being natural in his estimation that the town was strictly for white folk, especially after dark. The irony in this prejudice, he being the direct descendent of a full blooded Cherokee, was lost on George. He wasn't big on irony. I was surprised, Illinois being the home of Lincoln and in the 'north' or so I thought even then aged ten. By his account, rural Illinois was not much different from rural West Virginia, Tennessee, Alabama or Georgia.

He told us of his pack of American hound dogs and the guns he had and the hunting for deer, possum, quail and squirrel, their main weekend activity in season and probably, knowing George, out of season as well if the larder demanded it. He told us of cousins and a sprawling family that spread over much of that part of Illinois; of girls and conquests, of High School and its failings. It had certainly failed him; he could only read and write with great difficulty.

Like many Americans, he was very generous. His GI wages were probably very meagre back in the USA economy but in postwar Britain they were in the upper middle class of earners if not in manners. Besides which, they had the PX store at the base where they could buy most of what they needed tax and duty free which made their wages go even further. American chocolate bars, whiskey and cigarettes were pennies to him and he invested our house generously with them. I don't know if the PX sold anything else but if it did it was not of any interest to George who had a very limited range of, albeit great, appetites. We saw for the first time cigarettes in 200 cartons as they were strewn carelessly in the wake of one of his visits. True, they were American cigarettes, Chesterfields, Pall Malls, Camels and the like, but in those austere years no-one minded the harsh strength of them and they were gratefully consumed by an all-smoking household.

Smoking was an almost universal habit then before the medical profession recognised the danger in tobacco. All our heroes smoked in the films. My God, even top sportsmen smoked! The only constraints on universal smoking that I can recall were that women were not supposed to smoke in the street –

'Look at that brazen hussy with a cigarette in the street! An' ah thought she were well brought up. Common as muck. 'Er mother 'ud be proper ashamed. 'Ere, gi' me a light, Kath,'

– and you didn't smoke on the downstairs of double-decker buses. Upstairs on double-deckers, you could barely see a hand in front of your face, and if you couldn't afford your Woodbines one morning, you just needed to take the upstairs deck and get your fix vicariously. Not surprisingly at aged eleven, I thought it was the smart thing to do, and cigarettes were all too readily available, so I smoked. My mother, a smoker herself, readily condoned it but, not being sure of Father's reaction, I hid it from him. Of course, he knew. On my sixteenth birthday, when in theory it became legal, he casually offered me one of his, and I casually accepted, both of us tacitly acknowledging the past five years' habit but him still making his subtle point about The Law.

Sometimes George and his buddies would get drunk mid week in the afternoon. This was always during the periods when he was a Staff Sergeant and not busted down to Private and therefore in charge of his small team of mechanics and, of course, when the Colonel was away. He once arrived at our house in the late afternoon with three of his buddies packed into a Morris Minor, owned as a joke by one of them. How the hulking Yanks managed to get into a Morris Minor is a tribute to the vast quantity of Canadian Club rye whiskey they had already consumed. Each had his personal bottle and they drank straight from the neck as they roared and laughed inside the airless Morris Minor. After a little while parked up outside the house, they fell to debating the abilities of the ridiculous little car they were in and the owner, a wiry little Mexican, was so affronted by the insults of his three companions directed at his little car that he made them a bet. He bet it would take all of them up the steep grassy embankment separating the service road from the trunk road. Oh, the power of whiskey on a man's judgement!

The bet was enthusiastically accepted and so the little car was manoeuvred broadside across the service road and backed up as far as possible to get the best run at the challenge. With whiskey roars of encouragement and engine screaming the car shot across the road, bounced across the curb and managed to get halfway up the embankment before coming to a halt, engine screaming for mercy by now and clutch billowing clouds of blue smoke in protest. All the Yanks now bounced up and down in a vain attempt to get the little Morris Minor to complete its task, but it was futile and the men, being good, if drunk, motor mechanics, recognised the imminent mortality of the car and gave up. The weight distribution of two enormous Yanks in the back seat and one enormous Yank in the passenger seat but with a wiry little Mexican in the driving seat, together with the steepness of the embankment, meant the front wheels were teetering off the ground and the whole thing was in danger of toppling backward down on to the service road. So they let the little car roll back down the embankment and George got out laughing and shouting to his buddies as he weaved his way down our path. Miraculously, the Morris Minor was still able to drive and even more miraculously the three remaining Yanks were able to pilot it off into town to complete their carousing.

Fortunately, I was alone at home to enthusiastically witness the whole of this episode; otherwise I don't know what my mother and father would have done, but they would certainly have stopped it. But George wasn't finished yet. Filled with bonhomie and Canadian Club, he insisted I try the delights of rye whiskey which he was well familiar with by my age. I, of course, was all for it. If this magic drink could make people as happy as I had seen them, and encourage them to daunting but entirely wonderful feats like driving a Morris Minor up the embankment outside then just pass me the bottle! I took a long hard pull from the bottle and swallowed. My mouth, throat and stomach burst spontaneously into flames and I was sure that smoke was billowing from my ears and any and all orifices. As I gasped for breath and danced frantically round the room, George roared with laughter and encouraged me to take another swig. But I was still disabled from the first swig and not likely to repeat it any more than poke red hot needles in my eyes.

George had a solution. He recognised that whiskey tasted strange the first time, he said.

'Strange? STRANGE? It tastes worse than a Chinese wrestler's jockstrap set afire with petrol!' I wanted to say but still couldn't.

'Yeah, what you need to do is eat some apple with it, then it won't taste so bad. You'll soon get used to it. You like apple, don't you?'

Urged on by George and still lured by the attractive influences of the magic liquor, I tried some apple. It helped with the burning and it took away the worst of the whiskey taste. And so I was introduced to the joys of whiskey. A good bite of the apple then a good swig from the bottle and soon I was drunk as a skunk and George and I enjoyed a deeply intellectual discussion of the type that can only be had between one drunken bum and another.

> The wonderful love of a beautiful maid,
> The love of a staunch true man,
> The love of a baby unafraid,
> Have existed since life began.
> But the greatest love, the love of loves,
> Even greater than that of a mother,
> Is the tender, passionate, infinite love,
> Of one drunken bum for another.
>
> Anonymous but much used by Alcoholics Anonymous, I am told

Then my sisters arrived home from work and immediately recognised the calamity of the situation if Mother was to arrive home and see the same thing as they – George in deep conversation with their eleven-year-old brother, both deliriously, happily drunk and the brother incapably so.

'George, you big silly bugger, why have you got David drunk?'

'Gee, he's a good kid and it's time he got drunk and had a good time,' said George happily.

'Me mother's due 'ome in 'alf an 'our, what's she gonna say when she finds 'im like this? She'll go bloody mad an' you, you big daft sod, you won't be allowed within a hundred miles of 'ere.'

The enormity of the impending disaster finally penetrated George's Canadian Clubbed brain and even I sensed a slight difficulty.

In a way, I solved their first problem. Having paused in the apple/whiskey feast, and sensing some big problem from the horror in my sister's eyes, now spread even to George's, I suddenly felt very sick.

'Outside, Dava, outside! For God's sake don't do it in 'ere. We'd ne'er get rid of the smell.'

And with that plea ringing in my ears I was hustled outside to the bottom of the garden, heaving and groaning as I went. The remaining whiskey-soaked apple contents of my stomach were projectile vomited onto the back field and I settled back on the stone path to have a pressing and deep sleep.

I learned afterwards how they had managed the situation after my lapsing into blessed delirium on the back path. My sisters had cleaned me up and George carried me upstairs to bed where I was undressed and covered up. They told Mam I'd got a really bad tummy upset, I'd been sick and they had put me to bed.

'Ee, 'e were right poorly, Mam, poor little bugger. Somethin' 'e ate ah expect. Anyway, 'e were sick and such then he wanted to go to bed so we settled 'im in an' 'e's fast asleep now. I w'un't bother him if I were thee. 'E'll be all rate in the morning.'

And I was, and a friendship with the demon whiskey was formed that lasts to this day.

Dorothy had met George in a Doncaster pub on a Saturday night when he was out carousing with his buddies and, given the genetic Fanthorpe women attraction to the exotic, had befriended him. Dorothy was a 'bit of a lass'; otherwise she wouldn't have been out in the Doncaster pubs at the weekend, a source of many rows and recriminations in our house because Father had expressly forbidden it. She did it nevertheless, headstrong and defiant as she was and remained all her life.

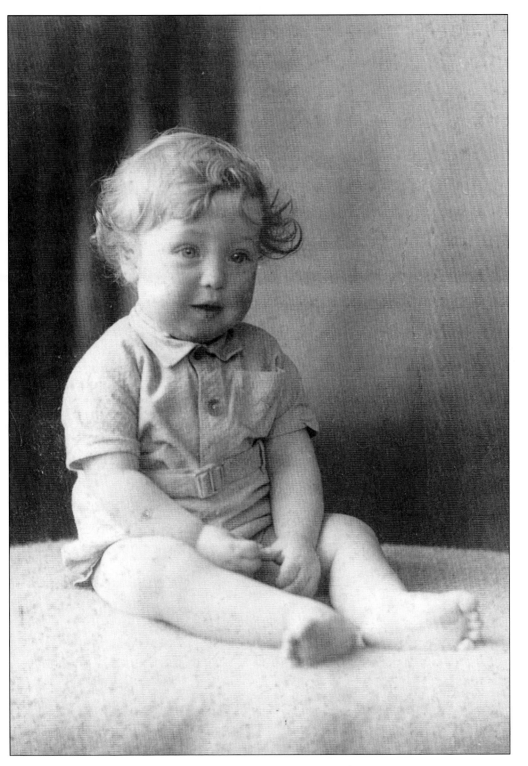

1. Little Tyke – aged about nine months

2. Little Tyke – aged five

3. Brother Douglas – Bombardier 19076040. Dortmund, Germany, July 1947

4. *Little Tykes — Michael and me, Balby back garden 1949*

5. *Little Tykes — Michael and me, July 1949. Our trousers were made from now redundant black-out curtains*

6. My mother the then Kathleen Umpleby in 1925. Who did she send this picture to, with love?

7. Mam and Dad – Balby 1949

8. Coopers Street Party celebrating Armistice Day 1919. My mother and her sister Rhoda, 4th row up, 6th and 7th children from the right. My mother is on the left of the two sisters.

9. James and Kathleen the reluctant bride? My father and mother 1927

10. The fearsome Annie and George Umpleby, my maternal grandparents. Date uncertain but c. *1945*

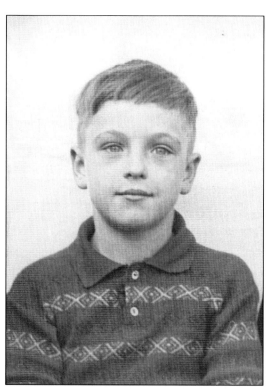

11. Little Tyke – 1950 school photograph, Wheatley Hills

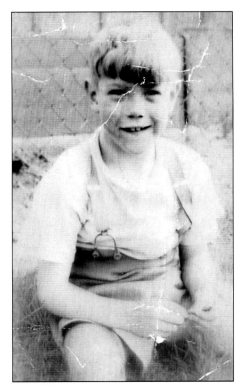

12. Little Tyke Michael. Back field, Wheatley Hills, 1950

13. Sister Marguerite and me, Wheatley Hills c. 1959

She was a bit of a stunner too was Dorothy and when she embarked on a Saturday night's foray painted, powdered and with stocking seams painted down the back of her legs with eyeliner in the absence of real nylons, I thought her the most beautiful woman I had ever seen. Not surprising then that she had no shortage of male admirers, but George being the alpha male among the GIs was particularly attractive and they courted or 'clicked' in the euphemism of South Yorkshire.

When she brought him home to meet the family, he was extremely respectful to Mam and Dad and generally on his best behaviour so the shock of it all was quite muted. Mam liked him and immediately sided with her daughter's choice and even Father grudgingly accepted that even though a Yank, George was a reasonable sort of chap and not necessarily the rampant despoiler of British womanhood that GIs were painted as, although only by the British male population (the female population being quite happily despoiled). He did have an almost childlike respect for parents and adults, common in many Americans, and it even charmed my father. This respect was genuine, having been born of the American practice of the dictum that 'there is a strong connection between the backside and the brain', certainly well practised in George's family by all accounts.

And so eventually they were married at St Mary's Church of England.

'A bit high if you ask me,' sniffed Father who, given his fundamentalist Protestant ethic, was always on the lookout for Roman deviances in the Church of England.

The reception was at the Fitzwilliam Arms, Granddad's local, where else, and was as happy and convivial a party as crates of Canadian Club, John Smith's finest Tadcaster Ale and a room full of rampant GIs could make it. Out of respect for George it was agreed that any fights would be postponed until after the bride and groom left so it was even brawl free until very late in the evening.

George and Dorothy eventually settled down in a rented house in South Elmsall, one of the many mining village satellites of Doncaster, and were very happy in those early years. George forewent his bachelor carousing and went carousing with Dorothy instead. They went to the fights at Doncaster Corn Exchange on Saturday nights where there was occasional good professional boxing and all-in wrestling when there wasn't boxing. They drank in the pubs as before and they visited 'Mom and Pop' regularly. George even took to taking Father out on his weekend off and my Dad loved the generosity and carefree-ness of the company. George didn't change his brawling habits though. Woe betide anyone who slighted his wife or newly acquired family, or for that matter threatened his alpha status among the fighting Americans. He and Dorothy were at the base one afternoon watching a baseball game. They were sat on the grass on a rug and George, who was always affectionate, kissed his wife. A passing RAF officer took exception to this uncivilised and very un-British public display of affection and advised George to take the lady behind the latrines if he wanted to do that sort of thing. Outraged at the implied insult to his wife, George leapt up, seized hold of the officer, who by now must have been seriously regretting his intervention, and escorted him to the latrines instead where he stuffed his head down the bowl and pulled the chain. A swift kick up the backside and the dripping officer retreated in search of the MPs.

George's weary Colonel on hearing the full story probably sympathised with the gentleman in George, there being not much love lost between the RAF and the USAF, so he duly busted him down to Private again rather than put him in custody for assault.

At the wrestling, they became good friends with one of the professional wrestlers, the Masked Avenger, or some such professional name, based on a mutual admiration of each other's fighting abilities and they socialised extensively in the pubs and bars of Doncaster when the Masked Avenger wasn't fighting. This culminated one night back at George and Dorothy's house in South Elmsall where they finished off the night's drinking after the pubs had closed. They fell to discussing the merits of each other's fighting skills, as you do, and eventually a dispute arose as to who would beat whom if they came to fighting. George was in no doubt and the Masked Avenger was in no doubt and so it seemed perfectly reasonable, as almost anything can after a bottle of Canadian Club, that they should test their varying opinion with an actual fight. So they did. Two hours later, with every stick of newly acquired furniture smashed to matchwood and each contestant at the point of drunken exhaustion George discovered that he couldn't beat the Masked Avenger and indeed, the Masked Avenger was beating him. Enraged and humili-ated, George jumped in his car to go to the Base and get a gun. What his fists couldn't achieve, a gun surely would. Dorothy thought for a long time what to do about this and in the end she did the right thing and called the Military Police. They were waiting for George when he returned with the gun and, taking no chances with their safety and that of others, beat seven bells out of him with their batons and threw him in the stockade back at the Base. Dorothy related all this to us afterward with the air of a slightly disappointed parent of a mischievous child rather than that of an enraged and angry wife. Such was their relationship. George was duly busted down from Master Sergeant to Private for the umpteenth time for that one.

George drove a six-cylinder version of the Ford Zodiac. It had been modified with two enormous exhausts which, at the flick of a switch, would shoot three feet of flame behind the car. This was achieved by temporarily strengthening the fuel mixture and adding a spark plug to each exhaust. We boys were massively impressed. George liked Michael and me because he recognised the same Huckleberry Finn spirit of coarse adventure in us and our dog-attended wilderness ways that he himself had practised and if truth were told, still did, for he was still an overgrown kid at heart. So he loved to show us stuff like his flame-throwing car. What the Doncaster Constabulary made of his car was never tested because he was unusually discreet with his flame throwing; the switch was never thrown when the bobbies were around.

In time, like all kids, he got bored with the car and swapped it for a 500 cc Norton motorcycle, probably the best model they ever made. The Norton was very nearly his undoing though. Returning to Doncaster one foggy Saturday after work at the motor pool, he disdained to slow down for the fog and collided head on into an oncoming lorry at 80 m.p.h. He was lucky he didn't die but he did sustain a horrific compound fracture to his lower leg which was smashed to fragments over six inches or so. It was touch and go as to whether his leg could be saved but after months of surgery and constant care, it slowly healed and he returned to active duty, much to Dorothy's and our relief.

Dorothy and George had a boy of their own by now, George Junior, and eventually they were all posted to Turkey by Uncle Sam, such were the needs of the developing Cold War at the time. George and family disappeared off, much to my regret, for George was a good pal of mine by then and I would miss him, my sister and their boy. Though Dorothy and her (by then) boys did eventually return,

George never did, and it was to be many, many years before I would see him again. So began my long affair with America and things American. Over-sexed, over-paid and over here was as good an introduction to Americania as you could get without joining the Rednecks in their natural habitat.

There was a serious postscript to my sister Dorothy's marriage to George however. Some years later, while I was enjoying my secondary education, Marguerite, the younger of my two sisters, left her Secondary Modern school at fifteen and joined Father on the railways as a telegraph girl. She had to learn Morse code because, believe it or not, train movements between signal boxes were still advised, one signalman to another, by Morse code telegraph. I remember helping her memorise the letters and testing her with the book she had been provided with by the railway company. It took a long time and at the end I was as proficient in Morse code as my sister, having learned it vicariously in the process.

Marguerite was an unusual girl in her teens. She was pretty in a plump and wholesome way, but shy and quiet and had few friends outside the family home and her immediate work environment. Partly as a consequence she and I grew closer as we grew older and shared the same taste in music and humour. Buddy Holly and the Crickets were the great musical love of those years and I still remember vividly being wakened at 6.30 in the morning by a distraught Marguerite, fresh from nightshift, with the news that Buddy Holly had died in a plane crash that night, 3 February 1959. She was inconsolable.

Marguerite had become a close elder sister, though she treated me as the older brother. Because she had no boyfriends, I would sometimes be enrolled to escort her out of an evening, when we would visit the pubs of Doncaster and take in some of the colourful Doncaster night life. We even went on holiday once to Torquay, courtesy of British Rail free passes which she received as part of her employment, and her wages which I began to look forward to as much as she did. Every pay day, I would be dispatched to the shops for sweets, fudge being a particular favourite. Then we would feast on the proceeds of her week's work until I felt sick, not being used to such cloying sweetness.

I often wondered about her apparent loneliness and her lack of interest in boys but I just concluded she was shy and not ready for that yet. I could never have guessed the real reason for her isolation.

Dorothy, George and their boy in the meantime had been posted back from the cold war front in Turkey to the USA in Colorado and I was envious of Dorothy's good fortune in experiencing the joys of US citizenship and culture, for the enjoyment of America was an ambition then of most young people. For us it was a place that only existed on celluloid but the celluloid told us it was invariably glamorous and everyone was rich or at least wanted for nothing. George and Dorothy had by now a second child, David Michael, who, I like to think, was named after my brother Michael and me.

Eventually Marguerite decided she would like to visit her sister and see America for herself. I was massively enthusiastic for her but Father was quietly but dogmatically opposed. I think he instinctively knew what I was only to discover to my utter astonishment some time later. There were some heated discussions in the house about this with me taking Marguerite's side and Mam, as usual in such situations, sitting firmly on the fence. Eventually, Dad gave up and Marguerite packed in her job and duly embarked for America. I was sad to lose a great sister but very happy for her opportunity. If only I had known.

Some months later, I returned home from work to find, much to my amazement, Dorothy and her two boys back home having arrived early morning and travelled up from Heathrow to Doncaster by train. I was told she was home for a holiday, and I had no reason to suppose this wasn't true though the suddenness of her arrival was perplexing. As the weeks rolled by and Dorothy remained, it began to dawn on me that something was up. Dorothy was depressed and withdrawn, sitting by the fire for hours on end, the inevitable chain-smoked cigarette dangling from her nicotine stained fingers. This was not like Dorothy. Eventually, the truth could be contained no longer. Dorothy had left George and for very good reason. He had taken up with Marguerite. Dorothy and he were divorcing so that he could marry Marguerite. I don't think I have ever felt so betrayed and so foolish. Father had been right all along and Dorothy and the boys were victims of my foolhardy support of Marguerite's visit to America. The house was scandalised, as well it might be, and Marguerite's betrayal of her sister was never mentioned outside the house, so neighbours wouldn't know. All they knew was that

Dorothy was divorced, scandal enough in those days, but well within the general expectations of a transatlantic marriage.

'I told thee no good 'ud come of it. Ya can't trust Yanks wi' marriage and women. Just look at that Errol Flynn.'

How true, though the fact that Errol Flynn was born in Tasmania of Irish descent somewhat diminished the argument.

Dorothy became increasingly embittered by her sister's betrayal, justifiably so, some would say, so much so that her whole life became blighted by her experience and she lived out her remaining years, it seemed to me, lurching from one disastrous relationship to another. She even turned her bile on everyone in her family at one time or another. She became a loud, hard line, unreasoning Communist in the process, a haven for many a disaffected and bitter character, and as a result became virtually unemployable. She even castigated me roundly and often in later years for becoming 'a manager' and therefore automatically joined to the hated capitalists as 'an exploiter of the working class and a running dog of a capitalist lackey' (she carried a pocket sized version of *The Thoughts of Chairman Mao* in her handbag). During one of these tirades, she spoke of Russia and extolled its virtues as a 'land of milk and honey', the irony of using a Biblical phrase to describe a despotic Communist state lost on her. She actually used those words, and that she wished she was there. Never one to miss an opportunity to call a bluff, I told her I would pay her airfare but with one condition. It would be a one way ticket only. She didn't take up my offer. Such was my relationship with her in adulthood.

Mam and Dad on the other hand, having just got rid of their brood, were left to pick up Dorothy's pieces and help raise two new children. They were two fine lads who have made excellent family men in their adulthood and I am very proud of them.

Dorothy died in 2000 aged sixty-seven of lung cancer, almost certainly caused by her relentless chain-smoking of the strongest cigarettes she could find. I was living in Florida at the time the news that she was ill came through and I wrote her a letter of reconciliation recognising it must be serious. I told her it was time to bury our stormy differences and recalled how she had been a great elder sister when I was a child. I remembered how I had once slipped one of my live white mice into her handbag just before she went out on one of her forays into Doncaster's night life, painted and powdered and as glamorous as ever on such occasions, this in retaliation for something that had happened between us earlier that day. Dorothy, to her horror, had found the live mouse when she opened her handbag to pay her bus fare some two stops into town. I recalled that her retribution was merciful, even muted for such an awful prank, and that that was typical of her relationship with me as a child. I wished her well and told her I would be home in a few weeks to see her. But it was too late, even for the letter, and Dorothy died before it got there. I didn't make it back in time for the funeral, my son David representing us. Dorothy's son asked David to read out my letter at the funeral breakfast and it was received well which was a relief and some comfort.

Marguerite did indeed go on to marry George and raise four children somewhere in the backwoods of Arkansas. They remained together, though in failing health, and Marguerite got religion, as well she might. She became a fundamentalist Baptist, common in the backwoods of America, and evangelised whenever the opportunity arose. She called me once and I caught up with her history. She worked in Bill Clinton's Arkansas State Governor's office as a secretary in Little Rock. At the time, Bill Clinton, the Governor, was running for President and I asked Marguerite if she would be voting for him out of loyalty to her employers. She was outraged. 'I couldn't vote for a baby murderer!' she screamed, a reference to his support of abortion. It was then I realised how deep the fundamentalist Baptist faith had gone. Before she rang off she said, 'David, I want you to find Jesus. Promise me you will.' I said I would and she gave me a few directions as to where and how I would find Him. No, Yanks are definitely not big on irony.

As for me, I was scarred by my naivety. I had learned that when it comes to people, there is ninety per cent more going on underneath than is visible on the surface, and if you must make a judgement, err on the side of caution lest what is going on underneath comes and bites your bum later. Marguerite's liaison with George must have certainly been born while he was married to Dorothy in England and it now explained an awful lot about Marguerite's shy and withdrawn ways.

But I had a new job in the challenging world of work and a new passion for learning and with the selfishness of youth I got on with it with gusto while the family suffered.

CHAPTER 6

Danensis

Grammar bugs,
Punch their lugs
Two for twopence ha'penny.

Local Doggerel

M Y NEW PRIMARY SCHOOL in the green and pleasant land, Park School, was as posh as the neighbourhood. It had playing fields and one of the teachers had a car. I settled in very well and I only have pleasant memories of the place. The teachers were vocational teachers as most were back then and they did a great job with the motley new intake of immigrants into Wheatley hills.

I remember charity drives when we were required to bring all the newspaper and cardboard we could lay our hands on or, on another occasion, milk bottle foil tops, all of which could be sold to raise money for the less fortunate in the world. I remember the school being piled high with newspapers and cardboard at the crescendo of the drive, with corridors and the hall lined with them and the smell of rancid milk that emanated from the box upon box of milk bottle tops similarly ranked throughout the school. The Head, a jolly and enthusiastic man, raised so much enthusiasm in us that no newspaper or bottle top was safe at the peak of one of our charity drives and many a man arrived home from his work looking forward to reading his newspaper after tea only to be disappointed by its mysterious disappearance.

'Bloody hell! 'Ave they got one of their charity drives at school again? Ah'll be bloody glad when all the starving in Africa are bloody well fed!'

I did well at Primary School, though not spectacularly well. That was reserved for the Headmaster's son, who was in our class, and a group of middle class children who came from the other side of Thorne Road in the 'owned' houses. I was in the top class but usually thirty-fifth or so out of forty and coasting along comfortably. Our household, though it had a reverence for learning, had no great expectations of its children or of the educational system other than to read and write well, do sums and know our history, so there was no great pressure on me, regularly delivering as I did these unambitious expectations.

But the 'Eleven Plus' examination was still in place then as Doncaster had a good Grammar School which selected its entrants and dispatched the rest to either Secondary Modern or Technical School education. I had no fear of any. I really didn't care where I went, and I had no expectancy of an Eleven Plus pass. That lofty ambition was for the top quarter of the class. But our teacher coached us all in the black art of exam passing as opposed to having the intellectual capacity to pass exams with nonchalant ease. He knew, as many have learned, that there is at least as much in the technique of exam passing as there is in regurgitating the headful of the stuff the examiners wanted to hear, or 'knowledge' as they would have it.

The day of the Eleven Plus drew near and it's a measure of my concern that the night before, I was out on a borrowed bike with Patch trying to see whether I could outrun his famous turn of speed with the mechanical advantage of a bicycle. I couldn't, but in a foolhardy attempt to outwit him, I tackled a hopelessly steep and rough track up a hillside, and in the process toppled backward, landing on the back of my head with a terrible thump. I still have the dent in my head to this day. Patch revived me with his enthusiastic licking of my face and I got up gingerly and tested first myself and then the bike for broken components. Apart from a terrible headache, I was unscathed but if I had harboured any secret ambitions of the following day's examination, they were surely dispatched now.

I went to the examination with a light heart and a thick head. There were the usual tests of our arithmetic, spelling and English skills, all of which we were well prepared for. Finally we had to write an essay on 'Advertising and its Effectiveness' which at eleven years old was a stretch for anyone. I was totally unconcerned and blithely wrote all I really knew about advertising, two sentences, followed by pages of my learned opinions on the merits of serious advertising versus funny advertising, the concluding thrust being that funny advertising was acceptable and entertaining, while serious advertising was boring and therefore unacceptable. It seemed reasonable to me at the time, and when the invigilator called, 'Pens down. Hand in your papers,' I was well satisfied with my morning's work.

Astoundingly, the examiners were too and in due course the magic piece of paper in a brown envelope arrived telling my parents I had been awarded a place at the Grammar School. At first, my parents couldn't believe it but eventually it sank in and there was immense pride in the house, particularly in my father who knew and secretly craved the opportunity this represented. My sister Dorothy was quite convinced the fall on my head the night before the exam was responsible for this outcome. She thought the fall must have shaken loose some brain cells which were lying dormant up to then but were now called up for Eleven Plus duty by the bump. She had a thing about my head, though, and its size relative to the rest of my body which was lithe with running, jumping and climbing all day long.

'How that great big head is held up by that little, thin narrow neck I do not know,' she would say, particularly after being the subject of one of my sibling targeted pranks. After Eleven Plus success Dorothy believed even more firmly that I was a massive brain carried about on two spindly legs and, of course, that little, thin narrow neck, such was her reverence for Grammar School.

After the jubilation, most of which went right over my head, worries set in. The Grammar School sent a long and exhaustive list of the equipment and clothing I was expected to arrive with and it was very expensive. I don't know how Mam and Dad did it, but the money was raised and I was traipsed round the Grammar School appointed stockists for the uniform, including a ludicrous red cap and a tie, the sports gear ('Must be in Easterfield House Colours') and all the geometric equipment required for an upcoming Euclidean mathematics education. In all my eleven years I had never, not once, worn a tie, let alone a cap. The nearest I had come to a tie was to use an old one of Dad's to help lash together our go-cart/dog combination. But the rules of the school which came with the ruinous list of purchases demanded that when in the street in school uniform, I MUST wear cap and tie. It began to dawn on me that I was entering an institution that was the very antithesis of my Huckleberry Finn existence, especially if I was required to walk the streets of Doncaster with a bloody red cap on my head. Oh, the shame I anticipated from this! There was an old piece of children's doggerel that I had sometimes used to bait the unreasonably privileged Grammar School boys we came across, only occasionally since there were none in my neighbourhood. It was based on pure envy and disdain for anything or anyone fortunate to have any sort of privilege. And it was a defence mechanism that allowed us vagabonds to feel good about our station in life and raise it to a privilege itself.

> Grammar bugs,
> Punch their lugs,
> Two for tuppence ha'penny.

It said it all. They were effeminate effetes who couldn't fight, were little better than insects and for all that, not worth very much. Children do have a way of getting to the heart of the matter. It wasn't true of course. These taunts were always proffered from a safe distance since the Grammar School boys were always much bigger than us primary school kids and were very fit from the rugby and athletics programmes that were enthusiastically pursued at Grammar School.

So it was with some trepidation that I approached the first day of term at my new school. I was astounded. 'Doncaster Grammar School, Founded in 1350' said the proud notice at the front entrance. You'd have thought they might have thought of something better by now, I thought. The teachers all went about in cap and gown and if I thought my new red cap was ridiculous, the mortar boards were even more so. The Headmaster was a Doctor (of Divinity, whatever that was). There was a library and vast sports fields. There were squash courts (though defunct now and only used for smoking, I later discovered), swimming baths and a Railway Society which was endowed with an enormous landscaped scale model train set housed in the school tower where the Society club room was located, this a tribute to the town's railway heritage. All the teachers were men; in fact there was only one female in the entire school and that was the school secretary, if you didn't count the dinner ladies, and Doncaster Grammar School didn't.

There were so many classrooms I couldn't count them and there were even lecture theatres with benches rising from the front to the back either to help the student see the lecturer the better or probably so the lecturer could see the student all the better. In these rooms we were to be taught subjects I had never heard of as well as the ones I was all too familiar with; physics, pure mathematics (as opposed to applied maths roughly defined, I later learned, as pure maths sullied by commerce and industry), ancient Greek history, geometry, trigonometry, divinity, Latin, and later, Ancient Greek language. And we were to be taught each subject by a different teacher in a different classroom in groups of thirty or less!

There was also a whole half day set aside for sports, although the school week was extended to include Saturday mornings to compensate. This was clever scheduling by the sports-mad Headmaster who figured if the school sports were on Saturday morning, as in most schools, only sports zealots would turn up, so he scheduled sport for Wednesday afternoons as part of the syllabus, with Saturday morning as a standard teaching morning so even the 'sick, lame and lazy' had to take part, much to the many adolescent couch potatoes' disgust. This was altogether a world whose customs, practice and knowledge I had absolutely no comprehension of until that first amazing day and I got stuck into it with gusto.

The lessons were rigorous, the masters demanding and there was usually two hours homework at night after the labours of the day. My form master made it clear that from the primary school reports he had access to I had not been expected to pass the Eleven Plus and that I had the place of some very able students who had not passed including the Primary School Headteacher's son who must have had a bad day and was consigned to Technical School.

Aroused by this patronising and calculated needle, I set out to prove that the Primary School assessment was wrong and that my sister's impression of my brain size and power was correct and I worked like a Trojan all year on the strange new subjects.

I rapidly gained the impression that the Romans were still in charge and had never gone home since Latin was ever present. The physics master even taught us the rudimentary laws of science in Latin:

'*Ut tensio sic vis!*' he bellowed of Hooke's Law of Springs. 'As the force, so the extension!' he translated for us which was just as well since we hadn't the faintest idea what he was talking about.

I wondered about this. All of the laws we learned at this early stage were laws discovered and defined by fine Englishmen, Hooke, Boyle, Newton and the like or Scotsmen at the very least. All things fine were British at Doncaster Grammar School since they saw themselves still as an integral component of the British Empire and a supplier of quality manpower for the Foreign Service. Surely these fine British heroes of science defined their laws in English? Apparently not; Latin, we were told, was the language of scholars and gentlemen across Europe in the seventeenth, eighteenth and even nineteenth centuries and we were being steeped in it in the (largely vain) hope that the 'gentleman' and 'scholar' would rub off on us. Since most of us couldn't even speak a version of the Queen's English that anyone south of Nottingham could interpret, this was ambitious to say the least.

'Whats tha' reckon t'this Latin then?'

'Buggered if ah know. It's all a foreign language if tha' asks me.'

The history lessons were of the Roman Empire and its philosophies and methods and its bloody wars of conquest and how it assimilated the native populations by brute force after conquest. Strange, then, that the very first Latin verb we were taught was '*amare*– to love'.

Romans – love? No, I don't think so.

Romans – fight,

Romans – slaughter,

Romans – conquer,

Romans – stab each other in the back in public.

That's more like it!

Nevertheless, *amo, amas, amat, amamus, amatis, amant* were the first words we uttered in Latin as we conjugated the verb to love. Come to think of it, it was the first conjugating we ever did, never having heard of that before either.

We learned that Doncaster was founded by the Romans, who called it Danum.

'Why is it called Doncaster then, Sir?'

'Because it was renamed by the later Saxons, boy.'

'Why did t'Saxons call it "Doncaster" Sir?'

'It means "Camp by the Don" in Latin, boy.'

'But why did t'Saxons call it a new Latin name when it already 'ad one, Sir?'

Sir, wearily but with a threat of violence in his voice: 'Because, stupid boy, they were gentlemanly and scholarly Saxons. Now let's get on!'

It follows that the citizens of Danum were Danensians and since we were all current citizens of this wonderful town founded by Rome's best and even refined by scholarly Latin speaking Saxons, then we should endeavour to keep the language alive and sing our school song in Latin. It started with a rousing crescendo of 'Danensis! Danensis!' and went on to extol the virtues of Doncaster Grammar School in much the same style that Virgil might have used if he had been foolish enough to venture this far north in the Roman Empire to sample the delights of Danum. I never did discover what those virtues were, however, since the translation was beyond me even in later years. Ah, but ask me to conjugate the Latin verb 'to love' in the present tense . . .

Latin, French, pure mathematics, geometry, English language, English literature, physics, chemistry, geography, divinity and art – I laboured mightily on all these subjects that first year, and with great results. In the year end examinations I was in the top ten for the whole year in all subjects, which was important because they used these results to begin streaming us in the second year. My form master professed his surprise and added his congratulations though he could barely conceal his disappointment given his faith in the primary school Head's judgement over that rendered by the Eleven Plus.

On reflection, the one subject that was significant for its absence was biology. I don't recall that we did biology. This was almost certainly because it avoided the need to talk about the female sex and some of the nasty practices that could be enjoyed therein. Girls, women, were never mentioned at DGS. It was as if they were an undiscovered species as indeed they probably were to at least some of the Grammar School masters. It left us free to speculate (some would say fantasise) wildly as to the nature of 'women'. But this being a single sex Grammar School, these speculations would have to wait some years before being put to the test.

If women were explicitly missing from the curriculum, this was made up for in English literature where every poem we studied seemed to involve beautiful women in some distress and often undress. There was 'The Rape of Lucrece' by Shakespeare:

'Sir, Sir! What's rape?'

'It means to seize or carry off from the Latin *rapere*, boy.'

'Oh, right, Sir,' disappointed, 'only me Mam was wondering what sort of stuff you were teaching us when ah took it 'ome for 'omework.'

> His hand, that yet remains upon her breast, –
> Rude ram, to batter such an ivory wall! –
> May feel her heart-poor citizen! – distress'd,

Wounding itself to death, rise up and fall,
Beating her bulk, that his hand shakes withal.
This moves in him more rage and lesser pity,
To make the breach and enter this sweet city.

William Shakespeare: 'The Rape of Lucrece'

So that's what the despicable cad Tarquinius did. He 'seized' Lucrece. It didn't read like that to me, though with a vast stretch of imagination, there was a bit of seizing going on there.

Then there was 'Christabel' by Samuel Taylor Coleridge.

Beneath the lamp the lady bowed,
And slowly rolled her eyes around;
Then drawing in her breath aloud,
Like one that shuddered, she unbound
The cincture from beneath her breast:
Her silken robe, and inner vest,
Dropt to her feet, and full in view,
Behold! her bosom, and half her side –
A sight to dream of, not to tell!
O shield her! shield sweet Christabel!

Bloody hell! Never mind shielding sweet Christabel, there were thirty prurient boys needing a bit of shielding. I suppose the school believed that if physics was best taught through Latin, then sex education was best taught through classical literature. Neither theory proved correct.

Given that this was a haven of classical literature, of Virgil and Shakespeare, of Caesar's Wars in a desert of commerce and industry, coal mines and steel, you would have thought the graffiti would have been of a much higher class, witty, urbane; in Latin perhaps or even Greek. But no; it was as coarse and vulgar as the land outside the gates of The Haven. But it must have had some merit in wit or composition because I still remember some of it even now.

In a neat hand on the toilet door:

These bloody bogs are no good at all,
The seat is too high and the hole is too small.

Under that, in a different hand:

To this I must add the most obvious retort,
Your arse is too big and your legs are too short.

And in yet another hand underneath this, sardonically:

Who would have thought with all his wit?
That Shakespeare came in here to shit.

And so I entered the second year in the 'A' stream in 2A, and all was well.

Then disaster struck. After roaming Sandalbeat Wood one Sunday morning, we were weaving our way slowly back to civilisation for Mam's Sunday dinner, Michael, Patch and I when, at the very edge of the forest, where wilderness reluctantly gave way to civilisation, we came to the stream, about eight feet wide. There, someone had thoughtfully hung a rope from an overhanging branch and you could swing from bank to bank Tarzan style. It avoided having to use the footbridge about a hundred yards downstream. That was for sissies anyway. We took it in turns to swing backward and forward across the stream for half an hour or so, as you do, when, in mid swing and stream the branch broke and I plunged headlong into the mud at the bottom of the shallow water. My leg locked firmly into the mud but my forward momentum carried my body forward at high velocity, such was the enthusiasm of my swing, and my leg broke at the femur. Michael says I was ranting and raving with the pain and the shock, but being a Grammar School boy, I was shouting Shakespeare at the top of my voice. If I had been a true Grammar School boy, my ranting would have been in Latin. I remember nothing of that, but I do remember a man running from the allotments to see what all the furore was then dragging me from the stream bed with outstretched arms, my broken leg bumping along behind me over the rough ground. Michael left me there to summon help with Patch whining and fussing and willing me to get up and carry on with the game.

As luck would have it, my father had been working on his allotment that morning only a few hundred yards away. He wasn't there however; since lunchtime was near he had retreated to the working men's club over in Intake. Michael eventually found him there and with wild panic told him of my plight. Father and Michael rushed back and Father confirmed Michael's diagnosis and he set to work applying his St John Ambulance Brigade skills, having roundly cursed the Good Samaritan for pulling me from the stream bed without a splint. He had me in a makeshift splint in no time using wood and my silver buckled American belt that George had given me, then his own belt and Michael's too. The professional ambulance men, when they arrived, said Dad had done a great job and they carted me off to Doncaster Royal Infirmary still in my makeshift splint. Several hours of waiting in casualty (yes, it was the same then), an X-ray followed by a morphine shot and I was safely tucked up in bed in the men's orthopaedic ward, but this time in a Thomas splint, a medieval contraption made up of leg irons, sticking plaster and bandages that was firmly anchored to the bottom of the bed. As bad as the Thomas splint was, it was better than the alternative which was normally used for children, a spiker. A spiker was plaster of Paris from neck to tips of toes so that the whole body was immobilised, with, presumably, a small bum hole in it and a cod piece at the front, though judging from the smell that emanated from those who had lain in a spiker for two months or so, perhaps not. At thirteen I was thankfully judged to be old enough to do as I was told with respect to unadvised body movement and I was put in the adult version of this torture, the Thomas splint. And there I stayed for the next six weeks, suspended in my Thomas splint, the bottom of the bed on blocks so that my weight constantly put the broken leg under tension. They let me out then, my leg wasted, skeletal and totally stiff at the knee joint through inactivity, but only in leg irons, another medieval contraption that prevented any weight being put on the healing fracture but at least allowed me to get about under my own steam. When the ambulance arrived home, Patch, who had pined the whole of the six weeks, went crazy, hurtling about the house and running round in delirious circles wetting himself as he went, such was his delighted abandon at having his boy back.

Eventually, after another month of physiotherapy to get the knee working again, I was allowed back to school. I was almost three months behind the rest of the class and I struggled to catch up. In fact, I never did. Hormones kicked in and girls and a whole new world opened up and I slid slowly but inexorably down the class rankings, diverted by the amazing new world I was just discovering. When I was fourteen, Doncaster Grammar School and my father asked me what I wanted to do after leaving school as part of the school's career counselling. An engineer, I replied after some considerable prodding by Father, but in truth it was really his idea since I didn't care. Having personally experienced the wrecking of the railway industry and having made a strategic assessment of the coming technological age, Father reasoned that electricians were the future industrial aristocrats and that is what I should be. The school was appalled and considered this a total waste of their given education. I was dropped from Latin and pure maths and was consigned to applied maths instead. Clearly, Ancient Greek and the mysteries of the Classics were not going to be on my agenda. That suited me for I was tired of the old fashioned Grammar School ethos and its lofty artificial separation from the real world of commerce, industry and enjoyable vulgarity just outside the gates. It was an institution past its time and some few years later the people's republic of Doncaster, instead of reforming it and the Secondary Moderns, cast aside the six hundred years of Grammar School heritage and turned it into a Comprehensive School. At a stroke they deprived poor working class boys such as me of the superb educational opportunities that Grammar Schools represented.

At sixteen, I intellectually limped out of Doncaster Grammar School with six 'O' level GCEs, to the mutual relief of the school and myself, and into a job as a student apprentice with the Central Electricity Authority. Some would say I had not made the best of a Grammar School education, but as things turned out, I had taken enough from it to equip me for a profession that I was to enjoy immensely and enough to take enormous pleasures from literature and living. Back in those days, just having gone to a Grammar School with six gold standard GCEs opened a lot of doors that otherwise would have to be stormed. I'm grateful even now for all that and for the chance to be a Grammar Bug. The world of electricity awaited me and I couldn't wait!

CHAPTER 7

Best quality blue

Electricity is actually made up of extremely tiny particles
called electrons, that you cannot see with the naked eye
unless you have been drinking.

Dave Barry: 'The Taming of the Screw'

I STARTED WORK IN THE Electricity Supply industry in September
1958. I had got an apprenticeship after my father approached a
neighbour who worked as a charge engineer at Doncaster A Power
Station. Not many people will ever have heard of Doncaster A. It
was housed in a small Victorian building opposite the old swimming
baths in town, virtually anonymous in its Victorian disguise and small
as it was. In fact, it was a relic, having had a glorious past as the
town's first electricity supplier, but that was several generations earlier
before alternating current and it was now relegated to supplying the
trolley buses that plied routes all around town. Its role as town
supplier had long since been taken over by Doncaster B, conspicuously big and new across the North Bridge by the River Don which
served to cool its turbines, much to the river's obvious distress. The
Great North Road which ran through the centre of Doncaster once
had to be closed because the foam from the warm river completely
obliterated the road passing over the poor river.

When our neighbour invited me in to see the place, it turned out
that a charge engineer in such a modest place was a mixture of stoker,
turbine driver and maintenance man. But I knew nothing of the
proper status of charge engineer and was very impressed. I was
immediately smitten by the hum of the small turbines, the fires in the
boilers and the very fundamental industry of it all. It had symmetry
and logic and it was doing a very clever thing in my estimation,
producing as it did the mysterious, invisible but powerful electricity,
the power of all things new.

'Ay lad, best quality blue we make here,' said our neighbour and
the station's charge engineer.

So I went off to the interviews massively enthusiastic and full of
dreams of making the 'best quality blue' myself. I thought I was being

interviewed for an electrician apprenticeship, but the Yorkshire
Education Officer had other ideas given that I was a Grammar School
boy with six GCE 'O' Levels. Eventually I was taken on as a Student
Apprentice and indentured for six years to become a professional
engineer. Such was my immense good fortune for it turned out to
be a wonderful and rewarding experience.

I was assigned to Mexborough Power Station as my base and given
a highly comprehensive and structured programme of learning that
would stay with me for the rest of my life. The first challenge,
however, was to learn a new dialect as I struggled to communicate
with my new colleagues and instructors. Mexborough is a small
industrial town up the Don Valley from Doncaster with the steel of
Sheffield to the west, Doncaster and its railways to the east and
immediately surrounded by the coal mining industry of the Yorkshire
coal fields. Almost all the employees were from Barnsley or the
immediate mining villages, and despite their proximity to Doncaster,
spoke a very different Yorkshire dialect. I could barely understand a
word they said.

'Wiers t' laikin', Dayvid?' enquired an older apprentice from
Barnsley on my first day as I strode purposefully out of the fitting
shop, lump hammer in hand, oversized blue overalls scuffing the floor
as I went.

'Tha what?' I replied, bewildered.

'Wiers t' laikin'! Where are you working today ya silly bugger.
Don't you understand plain English?' he reiterated in exasperation.

'Ah, rate, ah've got thee now. On't boilers. We're replacin' t'chain
grate,' I said proudly.

Laikin', it turns out, is one of those multi-purpose words that the
Yorkshire dialect is scattered with. Roy Hattersley pointed this out
first in his book *Goodbye to Yorkshire* where he explains the various
meanings of 'Tha what'.

'Tha what?' – I am sorry. I didn't hear what you said.

'Tha WHAT!' – I am incredulous and I don't believe what you
said.

'Tha what' as in 'Give em tha what' – Administer a good thrashing.

And so on. The various interpretations are elastic and almost
endless.

'Laikin'' can mean working as in 'wiers to laikin'?' – Where are
you working?

Or, at the other end of the spectrum of meanings and confusingly, but correctly, it can mean 'playing' as in 'who're Yorkshire laikin' this week?' ('Yorkshire' used in this context *always* meaning Yorkshire County Cricket Club) – Who is Yorkshire County Cricket Club playing during this week?

It means both these opposites and almost everything in between depending on inflection and what it is combined with. So, a very difficult language and for several weeks I struggled to gain the new tongue.

Replacing chain grates on old boilers was a pretty terrible job, so naturally, a new apprentice fresh out of Grammar School was assigned to it with one of the 'heavy' fitters and his mate as a kind of social retribution for his past advantages. The Barnsley lads, all Secondary Modern and Craft Apprentices, relished that and never tired of asking with a smirk, 'What's tha' think of fittin' new chain grates then, Dayvid? Ah bet tha's never seen owt like that in thee Grammar School!' It was important for a new lad to bear this with cheerful fortitude, both the job and the ribbing, for otherwise you would be labelled as an incurable toff and a spoilt brat by the judgemental Barnsley rascals and by the Lead Hand and the Foreman if it came to that. It was no problem for me. I loved it. It involved feeding the cast iron grate off the end of its span and dismantling it chain by cast iron chain. It was filthy hard work with big lump hammers and blocks and tackle anchoring the remains of the grate so it didn't roll back under its own massive weight. The chain links were part smelted and burnt away by the year's fires they had endured since the last shutdown and sometimes they only came off their retaining rods by hammering them mightily with the sledge hammer. Every strike of the hammer would raise vast clouds of acrid dust from past ashes which got everywhere, so naturally I was given the hammer when it was needed to remove the links and required to take the dust. My brand new navy blue overalls issued by the storeman ('They're too big' – 'Nay, tha's still growing, at least Ah hope tha' is, tha's no bigger than a bantam. Tha's a right little Tyke.' I learned never to argue with the storeman; he's a very important man when you need something, a good friend in need but a terrible enemy if you got on the wrong side of him) were soon a mottled grey, the bottoms scuffing along the floor and the metal buttons glinting out of the layers of dust. This was real engineering, I thought, and besides which I had always loved wanton, forceful destruction with lots of dirt and now I was getting paid for it! (58 shillings per week, the very bottom of the National Agreement pay scales, but a treasure trove to me then). Occasionally, the fitter would take pity on me in the afternoon, and tell me to take a rest.

'If tha' lays under t'grate wi' thee feet stickin' out o' the inspection door tha' can 'ave a nice little kip an' if that miserable bloody Foreman comes by ah'll gi' thee a kick. 'E'll never know,' he would say.

In truth I needed these rests for I was up at 5.30 a.m. to get to Mexborough by 7.30 and the work and hours were physically demanding for someone fresh out of school. But I was toughening up fast. You had to in order to maintain any sort of credibility with the rest of the lads.

The Barnsley lads were a great bunch, dry in wit, frank, direct and honest in their speech. Generous in their comradeship, they soon took me into their fold. I had a sort of ranking in their pecking order because I was 'educated', a Student Apprentice rather than a Craft Apprentice, I had taken my various induction rituals cheerfully like a man, and, very important this, I never alluded to any sort of superiority. In their society status could be given, grudgingly, but never claimed.

They were also generous enough to take the mickey out of their own Barnsley culture and they had a fund of stories involving Barnsley characters of note. My favourite, which I still remember, is of the Mayor of Barnsley, the Mayor being in a humorous category all of his own. The story went that the Council was discussing a proposal to add a gondola to the town lake. After much discussion in which large costs were quoted, the Mayor, who was presiding over the meeting, finally intervened saying, 'If it's going to cost that much, I vote we buy two and breed 'em. That way we'll make a bob or two.'

I'm sure the story was apocryphal, but the Barnsley lads roared with laughing at their own cultural shortcomings; but as a Doncaster lad, I had to be careful not to enjoy these stories too loudly or obviously lest Barnsley became defensive.

They loved their mothers, Yorkshire County Cricket Club, drinking Barnsley Oakwell Ales when they could afford it and Barnsley Football Club – not necessarily in that order. Their prime love depended on the sporting fixtures so it was Yorkshire when they were playing Lancashire (or for some reason Surrey – 'Southern ponces!'), Barnsley FC when they were playing Doncaster Rovers or either of the Sheffield clubs, and their mothers every night when they went home for their tea or wanted washing doing outside of the normal Monday washday for some reason.

' So I was assimilated into their society and because I had a natural inclination for it, I organised the various events the apprentice association was expected to get involved in. We went on a riotous trip to the Dagenham Ford Plant which was genuinely enjoyed for its technical educational value and even more so for the coach ride down and back with crates of Barnsley Oakwell Ale. We went to the Manchester studios of ITV and *Coronation Street* and on a trip to the English Electric turbine plant at Rugby, all enjoyed in much the same way. In the summer we all went to Butlins Skegness for a week's holiday, though I hadn't organised this; it had been booked a year in advance. For me it was the ultimate mark of their acceptance and they even changed the booking so I could go at the last minute.

'Tha'll 'ave to get thee washing done t'neet, Dayvid, we're off tomorrow. Slip thee Mam a few extra shillings, she'll do it fo' thee.'

And so it was. Mam happily washed my only good shirt without the need of a few extra bob and pressed my only suit and I spent a boozy, laughing week at Butlins Skegness though it could have been anywhere since I don't recall ever seeing the sea.

I played in their annual twenty over cricket match with the management, and though I wasn't much good at cricket, Doncaster Grammar School having given up on me at cricket very early ('No, no! Keep the bat straight, boy! Oh you are hopeless, boy, go and learn how to score.' How can you keep the bat straight when you're trying to knock the skin off a ball that's trying to take the skin off you?) I survived without any ridicule for my two allotted overs of slow right arm over the wicket because I bowled to a good length, or so the first of my two clean bowled victims said ruefully, although I wasn't aware I had any conscious control over where the ball pitched. When batting it also helped that they played a curious rule change from standard cricket in that no LBWs were allowed. This was apparently because some years before there had been a terrible row over an umpire's LBW decision which resulted in the apprentices taking their ball home with accusations that the umpire, an electrician's mate, was toadying up to the managers. So anything that looked a bit dodgy could be padded away, though that didn't help much if you were in a run chase.

The cricket was taken very seriously but the real value was in the opportunity for the lads to mix socially with the station managers, who were good men and close to their employees in such a small station. There was little formality beyond the respect the managers earned just from being good engineers for that was the rule in the electricity supply industry and was enough to ensure they were addressed as 'Mister' by lowly apprentices. First and foremost, to be a manager, you were a good engineer with conventional management skills coming a distant second, even less than a second thought at interviews. After the match we all retired to the Ferry Boat Inn and everyone, managers included, got happily but not incapably drunk before the last bus home.

All the apprentices were required to attend Technical College on part time day release once per week. Most of them hated it, never recognising the dubious connection between academic engineering and replacing chain grates, but some had ambitions for at least a rudimentary engineering education. The majority were studying for City and Guilds craft certificates, but one or two had graduated to the Ordinary National course in S1, the first of three years to the full Ordinary National Certificate. They rarely got beyond S1, being content to retake it year after year until they completed their apprenticeship and were released from their weekly obligation to Barnsley Tech. They had a massive reverence for academic engineering though. They just didn't have the expectations of joining the elite of Ordinary National Certificate holders.

With the help of my GCEs I was enrolled in Second Year, Ordinary National S2 which immediately put me on a higher academic plane as far as the rest of the lads were concerned and I was often enlisted to help them with their course work. I loved the new subject matter and I couldn't wait to get back to Tech College each week and discover the next exciting instalment in the unfolding engineering story. I also enrolled in the Final Ordinary National Year, S3, for 'Heat, Light and Sound' (Physics to anybody else but Tech Colleges. I guess Physics sounded too grand for them) at night school. I would need it at some point as an endorsement to my electrical engineering qualifications in order to get into the Institute of Electrical Engineers, I was told. It meant trying to get the equivalent of 'A' level Physics in a year of part time evening classes and no-one held out much hope.

'You might as well start trying for it now; you'll need it before you get your Higher National Certificate in four years' time. It will probably take you those four years to get the Distinction the Institute requires,' the Education Officer said.

But I wasn't daunted by any of this, not even when I discovered that the lecturer at night school was my old physics master from Grammar School, who was doing some moonlighting to earn a little extra. After one term, the lecturer who had suffered my obstinate reluctance to learn physics at Grammar School took me on one side and said he couldn't believe the progress I was making and that I should get my endorsement with Distinction within the year. What was the difference, he asked? I told him that I was now learning with a purpose rather than just for learning's sake as at the Grammar School and the acquisition of knowledge made perfect sense now. He understood but he couldn't have known just how much I absolutely loved it all. I had found the first of my true vocations and I was revelling in it.

I passed everything that year with 80 per cent plus, including the physics, and the Regional Education officer told me I would now do S3 on a full time sandwich basis at Rotherham College of Technology to get not just an ONC but the Ordinary National Diploma. The Barnsley lads were in awe – 'Nobody's that bloody clever. Tha' must 'ave a brain the size of Headingly Cricket Ground!' they said and we all retired to the Ferry Boat Inn to celebrate after work. They were the most generous, genuine people I had ever met.

The fitters were a mixed bunch. There were the experts, people whose skill and knowledge of particular areas of the plant surpassed that of any others. These men were quietly admired and respected by all the craftsmen. Top of that particular bunch, and therefore of all the others, were the turbine fitters who could safely remove the turbine covers, uncouple and remove the rotors; reline, machine and scrape new white metal bearing liners and at the end of the maintenance, replace it all to within thousands of an inch. No wonder they were much admired. Then came the journeymen fitters, solid, dependable and well trained craftsmen but who were still gaining their experience. And bottom of the heap were the 'heavy mob', fitters who were not trusted with fine work and so did the heavy stuff like refitting chain grates and the like. They had often earned their meagre status. One had tried to fit a one and seven eighths inch nut onto a two inch stud, a clear impossibility, even with a flogging spanner and a sledge hammer, though he tried. This turned a simple repair on a pressure vessel into a major time-consuming job while the damaged stud was extracted and replaced. He took years of ribbing from his colleagues for that one. While the apprentices treated the turbine fitters with something approaching reverence, the heavy mob was treated with jocular familiarity, much as equals. When working with the heavy mob and the job met difficulties, the apprentices never missed an opportunity to ask with a smirk, 'Ah tha' sure tha's got t'right size nut?' or some variation on the theme.

So all this I learned too: respect for skills, knowledge and experience and that even though pay scales may say everyone is equal, this is never true. Just ask a turbine fitter or one of the heavy mob if he's mellowed by drink and inclined to honest self assessment.

The tradesmen all had a mate, fitter's mate, electrician's mate or instrument mechanic's mate. It was probably written into the National Agreement, this industry having been created by Attlee's post war government. With the socialist passion for central dictats on everything, whatever happened anywhere in the electricity supply industry was prescribed in agreements or standing orders. The mates were non time served and so were classed as unskilled in the National Agreement demarcation scheme of things, though this was a little unfair, the mates learning many of their craftsmen's skills as they went along. The fitter and his mate worked as a team on a regular basis so a working relationship grew up between them that was particular to each tradesman and reminded me of a kind of marriage. They generally got on well together but there were some underlying stresses and strains which surfaced but only fleetingly. I once was assigned to work with an electrical fitter and his mate. We were to service a big fan motor at the very top of the boiler, a good trek and climb from the electricians' shop. The mate carried the electrician's tool bag and we climbed up interminable steel stairs until we eventually arrived at our motor at the top and back of the boiler next to the outside windows, which was just as well because it was very hot up there and the open windows gave us some ventilation. The electrician set to work removing the covers, only to discover that he didn't have the right sized spanner for the nuts. The mate was dispatched all the way back to the shop for the spanner and half an hour later re-appeared, red faced and puffing from the hard climb with the required spanner.

'Ah managed wi'out it,' said the electrician, who had used the next biggest spanner in the toolkit in the mate's absence.

The mate, without a moment's hesitation, threw the hard got spanner straight out of the window to fall fifty feet into the canal outside.

'Tha won't be needin' that then, will tha?' he said without a trace of rancour, and the pair worked on as if nothing had happened.

I don't know whether it was in the craft training curriculum, certainly I suspect the Education Officer would have been a trifle surprised, but the older craftsmen took it upon themselves to give the apprentices their version of sex education. They took great delight in detailed questions as to their apprentices' sexual experience. Having determined that mine was more than somewhat lacking, thanks to the Grammar School's wilful neglect and my parent's mortification at even the thought, the craftsman I was working with at the time (one of the top men in the pecking order) proceeded to fill me in on the missing detail, from the mechanics of it to the female form and where things could be found. After a long pause while he lit and then drew heavily on his pipe, he finally added, 'Oh – and it's no good rubbing a virgin's bum.' Such was my shame at my ignorance that I could not bring myself to ask why this was so. I still don't know. But he was a respected expert so he must have been right. Such men could not be wrong though quite how he discovered and verified this is a mystery since 'as rare as a virgin in Mexborough' was a regular saying of the day to describe any scarcity.

The apprenticeship was designed to expose me to the widest possible power engineering experiences and after my basic craft training at Mexborough I travelled throughout the Yorkshire region and its power generating and distributing network learning new things as I went from grid control to transmission and central test and efficiency. But as well as the engineering I absorbed, I learned things that went unrecognised by me until many years later, about the society of work and its relationships, the real value of skills, whatever they were and the dignity of labour. What it didn't train was management and finance. Neither was ever mentioned in those six years of vital technical conditioning so I was unaware of even the existence of management science or of financial management, as indeed most of the industry was. When I once asked about man management, a grizzled old Maintenance Superintendent replied,

'Man management? Easy, that. Praise the good and bollock the bad. T'National Agreement teks care of the rest. That's all there is to it, lad. Now get on with thee work.'

In those days the title 'Manager' didn't even exist in the CEGB. You were Superintendent, or Charge Engineer or Officer. In retrospect it almost seemed as if the Board were frightened of an outbreak of unsanctioned management that might challenge the socialist inspired doctrine of central control in a nationalised industry. As for financial management, it was said that 80 per cent of the costs were for fuel, mostly coal at a price fixed to make sure the National Coal Board was viable, and the other 20 per cent hardly mattered. Money came from a bottomless central government pit so why account for it? For the time being, I stopped worrying about management, and 'got on with it' as I was ordered.

Periodically, I would return to a warm welcome at my base station at Mexborough and rejoin the comradeship of the apprentices and the engineering team. I was there during the Cuba crisis in October 1962. President Kennedy had ordered a blockade of Cuba to stop in-transit Soviet ships from delivering further strategic nuclear weapons to Castro's Communist regime and for a week the world teetered on the brink of nuclear holocaust when we would surely all have been wiped out, fried to a cinder, in the blink of an eyelid. It seems surreal now how we all accepted that this might, indeed, probably would happen sometime in the coming week as the Soviet ships steamed toward the waiting US blockade. We waited almost breathless. The electrician told all the apprentices that his generation had been and fought the last war, now we would have to go and fight this one. Ay, if we're not fried to a cinder first, we replied. The Soviet ships stopped at the last possible opportunity and the world breathed again. Armageddon was postponed at least until the next confrontation. How disappointed Uncle Ted must have been.

It was during the same base station visit that I received the worst upbraiding of my young life. I was on Control Room Training and the Charge Engineers would allow me to man the Control Desk for generator synchronisation and switching instructions from Grid

Control. I was sat tweaking an incoming generator turbine prior to synchronisation when the Station Superintendent came in on his tour of inspection. He talked to the Charge Engineer, a dour old Glaswegian Scot, ex Royal Navy ships' engineer and finally turned to me, my turbine having been put safely onto the grid and loaded. I remained seated while the Station Superintendent engaged me in pleasant conversation about my training and how I was enjoying it. I was in awe at the Station Superintendent. He was as powerful a man as I had yet met in the industry. Finally he left and I could tell from the Charge's red face something was bothering him. As the door closed behind the Super, he launched into me.

'The next time the Superintendent speaks to you, you dinna sit, you stan' up, boy!' he bellowed. 'You did'na give any respect, boy, and I will'na have that on my shift! Noo, get oot a ma Control Room!'

'But . . . but . . .' I started to reply.

'Oot, OOT!' he yelled, and I decided that discretion was the better part of valour and oot I went, humiliated and wondering what the hell I had unleashed in the fiery, dour and cantankerous old Scot.

I was going to tell him that far from lacking respect for the Super, I actually thought he sat on the left hand of God, the right hand having been spoken for, and that I had also been taught, at the Grid Control Centre no less, that when involved in the supervision of running processes or switching, you ignored all around you to concentrate on the job in hand, even if the Prime Minister entered the room. But I never got the chance and I slunk down to the river bank and, face in hands, pondered the ashes of my putative career, imminent Armageddon at the hands of the Russians and the filthy, reeking, steaming River Don as it flowed upstream from our cooling outlet to our cooling inlet. Nuclear holocaust was suddenly not quite so bad after all. Bloody hell! How could I put this right?

The Assistant Charge eventually caught up with me and said old Jock wasn't as bad as he seemed. Just let him cool off for a few hours, but be sure to catch him before the end of the shift. Get in first with an abject apology and a ready recognition of the depth of my sin and do it before he has a chance to say anything, he advised.

'Ah've worked wi' the miserable old sod for a year now and underneath that hard Glaswegian veneer beats a heart of pure clinker. 'Ee's a bloody good engineer though, an' actually, if tha can put 'is bloody Navy ways to one side, 'ee's soft about apprentices. If tha' does as ah say it will be rate, don't thee worry, lad.'

I took the good advice and applied it scrupulously half an hour before shift end. Old Jock had calmed down and he accepted my apology unreservedly. Nothing was ever said of it again and there was no mention of it in his report to the Training Officer on my training stint with him. I learned to like old Jock. The Assistant Charge was right about him. I was also learning so much that couldn't conceivably be described as power engineering, but things I would only be very grateful for in years to come.

I was also posted to Manchester for 'Manufacturing Training' at Mather and Platt, makers of boiler feed pumps, among many other things. It was there I met the love of my life, Annie who was a motor winder at Mathers. I saw her as I went about my various postings in the motor manufacturing section and was immediately smitten. But what immortal chat-up line would reel her in, I wondered. In the end after many furtive glances in her direction and she in mine, I plucked up my courage and strode across. 'Is tha doin' owt t'neet, lass?' was the best I could muster, the sheer presumption of it at first prompting Annie to feigned affront. We still laugh about it now but it was the unlikely start to a lifelong love. There were problems though. She was Catholic, daughter of Irish immigrant Dohertys, and I was Protestant as only my fundamentalist father could have made me. It didn't matter one jot to us, but the Catholic Church cared mightily in those days and so might my parents, I thought. Nevertheless, we got on with it and were soon living together at a time when such things were definitely not fashionable and in what seemed a short time, our daughter Julie was born. We rented an old two up, two down Victorian back to back terraced house that was little more than a broken down hovel in the backstreets of Newton Heath, North Manchester but it was cheap and we did the best we could with it. I commuted weekends back to Manchester from wherever I was posted and Annie went back to work at Mathers with Julie consigned to nursery while she worked to make ends meet. Marriage was impractical at least until we were older and some of the problems were ironed out but we didn't care.

Our street had a very colourful collection of characters. That part of Newton Heath was an Irish Catholic enclave in those days but there was the odd loud Protestant family scattered through the district, some of who made it their business to keep the old divide alive and well, especially on Saturday nights after a lot of beer. One in particular would come roaring drunk down the street at midnight banging and kicking on the doors demanding that the 'Catholic bastards come out and fight'. Eventually, his mother, a diminutive pensioner, would emerge in nightdress and curlers wielding a broom and chase him indoors, beating him about the head with the broom to subdue him which probably saved him from the Catholic men who might otherwise have made mincemeat out of him, but had more sense.

The house was a wreck. Once, while I was away in the week, the bedroom ceiling fell in onto Annie and sleeping Julie. Annie got it fixed by asking about in Mathers. You could get anything done cheaply round there, partly because no-one had much money and partly because it was the moonlighting capital of the world.

Annie's mother, Molly, stamped down the stairs one night and went straight through the floor at the bottom as the rotten floor boards succumbed to her uncompromising Galway farmer's gait. Moonlighters fixed it by filling it with concrete.

We had an old clothes mangle, there being no washing machine or spin dryer in those days. In the morning it was left against the wall opposite the window onto the back yard. By evening when you returned, it had migrated, courtesy of the gradient in the scullery floor and the vibration from passing traffic, right across the floor to come to rest at the back door.

The outside lavatory had no light so I banged a hole through the scullery wall quite easily using the fire poker because I had no tools and put an electrical supply through to give us light and for a while we were the proudest residents on the street, being the only people to have their night time offices lit by electricity.

We really didn't care about any of this. We bought cheap paint from Woolworth and painted and Polyfilla'ed inside and out so that by the standards of the neighbourhood, it was quite chic. The layer of paint doubled the structural strength of the place as a bonus. We were very happy.

In the meantime, I had completed the Ordinary National Diploma at Rotherham College of Technology with similar stunning results as before, 80 per cent plus throughout the subject range which considering all else that was going on was as much a relief to me as it was a surprise to the Education Officer. He was delighted, as was my base station ('Bloody hell! Did tha' 'ear about Dayvid? 'E got over 80 per cent in the OND! 80 per bloody cent! Ah reckon even 'is bollocks 'ave got brains in 'em!') and I was sent to interview for the new College of Advanced Technology at Bradford. This was a new concept in technical education in England, one of six nationwide set up by the Wilson Government as part of his 'white heat of technology' initiative. It was, they explained, to be a technology university and would specialise in engineering and technical education. Massachusetts Institute of Technology was to be its ambitious model. They intended to turn out not only first class engineers, but the complete educated man, they said. So English literature in the form of the modern novel, social and economic history, appreciation of art or music, psychology, economics and many others were included as complementary subjects in the curriculum, some of which would be compulsory and some of which would be offered as optional liberal studies. The course work would be on a six month thin sandwich basis for four years integrated with the apprenticeship practical training, leading eventually to an honours degree, if you were good enough. All students would have a personal tutor who would counsel and monitor both the course work and the practical training. I loved the concept and immediately lusted after one of the coveted places. But would I get one? They were interviewing GCE Advanced level candidates as well, and I expected them to get an easier ride into the new college. The very next day after the interview, I got a letter from the Education Officer at the CEGB saying I had been accepted at Bradford, and I would start in September. I could hardly believe the speed at which things had happened until it dawned on me that the CEGB knew I would be accepted even before the interview. They had fixed it and the interview had been a rubber stamp. No matter, I was in! And I had new reasons for ambition now.

CHAPTER 8

Colleen and college

College is a place to keep warm between high school and
an early marriage.

George Gobel

B RADFORD WAS A LOT HARDER than the Technical Colleges I had
been to. The class was the best that mostly Yorkshire could
muster, so the competition was fiercer; but that was stimulating. The
College judged that the Ordinary National entry was short on
mathematics while the Grammar School 'A' Level entry were not just
short on engineering, they had none at all, either practical or
theoretical. They certainly didn't have the advantage of beating chain
grate links with a sledge hammer for the last two years; they had been
safely ensconced in their respective sixth form common rooms
discussing Plato, Virgil and the rugger prospects that year. So in the
first year we were split. The ONC lads did extra mathematics and
only mechanical engineering, while the 'A' Level entry did extra
electrical engineering. The theory was we would all be on an equal
footing by the start of the second year when we would have a
common syllabus though it was a little obvious which group the
College thought would be the front runners. There was an easy
assumption that the Ordinary National lads would struggle with the
demanding mathematics while the 'A' Level lads would easily pick up
the engineering. To an extent it was true. The maths was very
demanding. It was the College's intent that we would do mathematics
to honours degree level over the full four years as an essential
foundation in electrical engineering and it set away at a cracking
pace. But at the end of the year examinations most had coped from
both groups and some had excelled. It was easy to pick out the real
intellects though. They did everything with a nonchalant ease and as
a result had time to enjoy the Students Union bar, get drunk and get
into all the other extra curricula activities that College life offered.
Three or four failed though and were promptly dropped by the
College who had a policy of evicting anyone who couldn't make it
first time through the end of year exams. No second chances. This

put the fear of God into all of us and there was much discussion about
what career to take up if you got thrown out. Curiously, nobody
expected to drop back into the National Engineering stream if the
College threw them out. The favourites in the event of failure were
to go into teaching or the police service! No wonder they both got
in such a mess.

I knew early that I wasn't one of the nonchalant intellectuals, but
I could cope by working hard. One lecturer, in pure electrical
engineering, even went so far as to loudly signal to the class whenever
he was moving into First Class Honours territory in his lecture
content and told us that if we had no such ambition, we could skive
off when this happened. I stayed and took his example to all the other
lectures. I had become determined to get one of their scarce First
Class Honours and I was prepared to work twice as hard as those with
the natural gifts to wrest one from them. And work I did. Not for
me the dubious pleasures of life outside the lecture theatres at
College. Every night and every waking hour I was steeped in
engineering theory, mathematics, physics, even nuclear physics. It
was a relief to get back to Manchester, Annie and Julie on Friday
nights. Here, I can't say enough in praise of the then CEGB. They
paid me my apprentice's wages even when I was at College. They
paid for the many essential textbooks, the College tuition fees and the
lodging expenses while at College. They even paid the travelling
expenses that got me to Manchester and back each weekend. And
they gave me an integrated practical exposure to power generation
and distribution in the six months away from College each year.
They were making such an investment in me that I couldn't do any
other than repay them with my best, even super-human, efforts, such
was my gratitude.

Despite the grindingly hard work I subjected myself to, I absolutely
loved it. Engineering in all its forms, physics and particularly the
mathematics I was now exposed to were literally mind bending and
I revelled in it all. I was thankful every day for the great good fortune,
for that is what it was, that had brought these opportunities to me.
And by dint of hard work and zealous enthusiasm, I was doing very
well in each of the year end exams and I thought I was at least on
track for the coveted First Class Honours. Through all of this Annie
went on working, with Julie in nursery, to keep house and home
together in Newton Heath and provide a weekend haven for escape

from academia. They don't come any tougher, feistier, more self-sacrificing and more enduring than lovely little Irish girls from the poverty and deprivation of Manchester's Irish ghettos. Thanks, Annie.

Lest I leave the impression that it was all work at Bradford, there were occasional riotous interludes. The lodging I was in in my first year was one of the old fashioned type that probably doesn't exist today. Every available space in the house was taken up by a bed and lodger and meals were taken with the family. This lodging had a motley crew of guests. There were four of us students, two young probationary policemen and a couple of Glaswegian steel erectors. One of the young probationers was a wild Irish lad from County Clare who, when afternoon shift was finished, would drink in the local pubs sometimes until the early hours of the morning with his policeman's privilege. He would then return to our lodging and rouse all the students out of their slumber to go drinking with him until dawn.

'Bugger off, Peter! I've got lectures in the morning.'

'No, no! Sure, you'll all be coming for a drink now. I know just the place! Don't be such miserable feckers.'

Sometimes this would be impossible to resist and we would pile into his Ford Anglia at two in the morning and career off to Leeds where Peter knew an Irish pub that stayed open all night, though blackout curtains gave it the appearance of any slumbering hostelry. Inside was the very opposite. Much frequented by policemen, exiled Irishmen and delectable (not for me!) Irish nurses, the place was heaving with merry customers, pints of stout in hand and great *craic* on their lips.

'Ah, 'tis Peter for sure. Come in, come in, Peter and wet your whistle. I see ye brought the student lads wi' ye. Welcome, lads, bar's through there,' said the enthusiastic landlord in answer to Peter's furtive knock at the back door.

And that would be that until six or seven in the morning when we would all pile back into Peter's Anglia and lurch back to Bradford, knock the milk bottles over on the step and grab a quick hour's sleep before lectures. Budget constraints and College demands meant these interludes were rare, but all the better for that.

There was also the Annual Rag Week when, with the consent of the authorities, police included, the students ran riot in the city in the name of charity. For a week, students conducted policemen on point duty, who duly pirouetted at the student conductor's baton command and one even sang. They lifted drain grate coverings and fished in the city centre and, of course, scaled the town hall clock and hung a bawdy message on it, all in the name of making people feel good because that was when they were at their most generous to our charity collections. Also typical of the stunts was an attempt to drink a pub dry. The Licensed Victuallers' Association enthusiastically endorsed the plan, as well they might, and the landlords agreed to make a generous contribution to the students' charity conditional on our success. The name of the pub was kept secret until evening opening time to prevent the landlord from craftily taking in extra stocks, which might have made our task all the more enjoyable but very difficult. The donation was dependent on our success at completely depleting the pub of alcohol. The great evening came and I went along to do my onerous duty, as you do. We took along a fellow student lodger who was the quiet and respectful son of a Welsh Methodist preacher. Up to then he had steadfastly refused our invitations to join us for a drink when we occasionally 'popped out for the last one', the strictures of his father and upbringing still governing his appetites and distaste for the demon drink. On this occasion he had been reluctantly dragooned in the name of charity under immense pressure from his fellow lodgers and was persuaded to take just a half pint as his contribution to the evening's effort. He did and went mad. He loved the taste, and more importantly its effects, so much so that we couldn't stop him. Within weeks of that fateful evening he had spent his entire term's grant on the demon beer and had to call home for an emergency supplement. Who said education was all about acquisition of facts? Education took many forms at Bradford, as living with policemen subsequently proved.

One morning over breakfast one of the policemen told us that there was an identity parade that morning in a case of indecent exposure. They were short of volunteers to make up the parade and asked if any of us fancied helping him out. We were all massively enthusiastic, but lectures prevented us from going, much to our disgust. One of the steel erectors, a nice lad, said he could do it and the policeman told him when and where he should attend. There was absolutely no selection in this, he just happened to be available and interested to go and see how these things were done. That night when we returned to our lodging it was to discover that the poor steel erector had been arrested and was still being held at the police station. The woman had picked him out for flashing her! The police gave him a hard time that day, he later told us. They wanted to know his whereabouts on a specific night some twelve months previously. Needless to say, he couldn't tell them at first; who of us could have? They browbeat him all day with entreaties to 'be a man for the first time and own up', but he couldn't. He hadn't done it. Eventually, in desperation, he was able to piece together his movements on that awful night and his movements and witnesses were able to provide a cast iron alibi and he was released. We students were outraged at the treatment of the poor steel erector. We remonstrated with the policemen who were totally unrepentant.

'He could have done it,' they said, 'and only volunteered for the identity parade to shift suspicion.'

The fact that it was pure chance that we weren't there in his place totally passed them by and they remained unapologetic. It was never quite the same after that and I had learned another life lesson about avoiding official contact with the police unless absolutely necessary.

And so I got to the fourth and final year. It promised to be even more demanding than the previous years and because it was going to need a lot of un-diverted work, I went into Halls of Residence instead of my usual and colourful lodgings. The Halls were great for study. You had your own small but well equipped room and there was a kitchen on each floor where you could brew up and meet your friends and make toast at any time if you wanted. Meals were provided in the refectory and the food was very good.

The course work proved very demanding. Transient and sub-transient network fault analysis, fourth, fifth and sixth order differential equations and matrix algebra and advanced nuclear physics were all in the final year syllabus (among many other things), subjects most engineers could only speculate vaguely about if at all. In addition, we were to do our own research project, externally assessed, which would count 40 per cent toward the final result. Tough, very tough.

On top of this, Annie and I had decided to get married as soon as finals were over and results were out. Not before time, some said. But I would be twenty-two years old; Annie nearly twenty-one and most of the obstacles had been resolved. The Catholic Church had finally and reluctantly agreed to marry one of its daughters of Christ to a Godless Protestant with several provisos spelled out in the Bishop's dispensation. Julie would have to be baptised into the Catholic Church, Annie would have to return to confession, Mother Church and Mass, and the Godless Protestant would have to have instruction in the Faith of Our Fathers. None of this was a problem for me and I sought out the College Roman Catholic Chaplain for my instruction. Once a week I went along for an hour's discussion with him about the tenets of the Church and how I should not try to change my soon to be wife, at least in her Catholic heritage. Eventually the formal stuff was all exhausted and we fell instead to easy philosophical discussions which I enjoyed. He was very relaxed and gave me a lot of leeway for being a fourth year student. He was also a converted Anglican so he understood only too well my childhood conditioning in fundamental Protestantism. I remember asking him about 'family planning', that coy expression for contraception back then. I was astounded by his reply for he told me that if I could truly believe in my heart of hearts that this was all right with God, then it was acceptable. I told him of my astonishment and that back in the Irish Roman Catholic enclave of Newton Heath I would be excommunicated for saying such a thing. Ah yes, he replied, but we are in the business of saving souls the only way that we can in an uneducated society like Newton Heath, which is to keep it simple and threaten with hellfire and damnation. There was a compliment to my educated status in there somewhere but I'm still astonished to this day that he actually said that back in the sixties when the Roman Catholic Church was so implacably opposed to contraception. At the final session with him I told him I really ought to go and do some swotting, finals being imminent. He said he would pray for my success and light a candle for me. I thanked him very much for his thoughtfulness but said I still thought study would produce a better result. He smiled and said,

'You are right. Go and study, my son,' and told me he would write to the Bishop to tell him of my successful instruction. I was now a bone fide Catholic wedding candidate.

The final year was proving every bit as tough as I had anticipated. My research project, automatic run-up and synchronisation of an alternator to the grid, was going in fits and starts. Eventually I was spending almost as much time on it in the evenings as I was spending on lectures in the day. But slowly, it came together and I set about building a working prototype from the then new printed circuit boards which I had to make myself, a motor/alternator set and a spaghetti junction of wires, contactors and any bits and pieces I could scrounge from the lab technicians. My tutor was massively enthusiastic, which helped, and he procured components that really should have been outside the College budget. At last the great day came when the much theorised and tested mess of wires, motors, amateur printed circuit boards and electronic detritus was to be commissioned. I couldn't wait any longer, I was running out of time and I still had to write up the whole of the research into a paper for submission to the external assessors. I chose a late evening when the laboratory was deserted and threw the switch that powered the motor/generator set. The tangled mess ticked and whirred, the motor/generator set came up to speed as if by magic and after a little technical prevarication from the electronics the contactor connecting the alternator to the grid crashed in and we were synchronised perfectly! I could hardly believe it. I shut the whole thing down, and then repeated the exercise. Same again! I must have cycled the contraption twenty times long into the night, such was my relief and even joy at the mess's effectiveness and I slept a little easier that night, late but content.

The draft of my paper was sent back to Mexborough for typing (strange how we take typewritten documents for granted these days) and it came back with profuse and generous praise from the Deputy Superintendent who had read it before passing it on to his secretary for typing. Mexborough was very, very proud of its very own scholar, which I am still touched by when I think of it today. The draft was perfect, with spaces left for photographs as I had specified, perfect that is except for one glaring typo repeated throughout. Strange for a power station secretary, but she had spelt 'turbine' as 'trubine' throughout. But that was soon put right and I had my research paper and a working prototype all ready for the external assessors, leaving me free to concentrate on a final push in the course work.

We started final examinations in blazing June weather. Two weeks of one per day stretched in front of us. It went reasonably well as best I could judge up to the very last paper, electrical engineering. I always left revision to the night and morning before an examination. It had worked for me for years. By the last paper, I was all but exhausted and I returned to Halls to revise the next day's subject after a particularly gruelling mathematics paper. I took out my electrical engineering course notes – two bulging folders of foolscap scribble and diagrams – and it suddenly dawned on me that there weren't enough hours between then and examination time the next day even to read the folders, let alone re-assimilate them. I panicked and began to read furiously. The faster I read, the greater the panic rose up until quite unbidden, I wanted to scream. It got worse. Eventually, I knew I would scream and there was little I could do about it. I put down the notes and ran out of the door to reach my friends on the next floor down. It would be OK if I could get to them before screaming. We had a brew of tea and I told them I had miscalculated the revision time required for the last paper. They all said the same and it didn't seem as bad. I went back to my room and even though it was still afternoon I slept until morning when I made some pretty judicious choices as to what would come up in the afternoon's paper and concentrated on those. I had made good judgements and it proved a relatively easy paper for that. If ever an experience proved the truth of that old management adage: 'Always remember the six Ps! Perfect Planning Prevents Piss Poor Performance,' this was it and I tucked it away for future example.

It was all over now and the anticlimax was at first delicious for its sudden, idle freedom. The Class of 1964 all went out together to a commandeered pub and we all got deliriously and very happily drunk. One of the last few things I remember of that night was a sweet, tiny old lady coming through from the bar to say how much she enjoyed our singing. She must have been deaf because the words to the Engineers Song are about as filthy, even disgusting, as a bawdy song could be. She retreated to a massed chorus of 'She's mine!' from the irreverent students, her congratulations ringing in our ears. The very last thing I remember was seeing one of our number, one of the 'nonchalant academic ease' lads, stretched out full length on his back on the bar with his arms crossed over his chest for all the world like an Irish wake subject and with a look of utter tranquillity on his face, lost to the world. I remember thinking how nice it would be to join him, and I did. Blessed oblivion.

The anticlimax was immense. Having spent four years with almost every waking focus on this moment, it was surprising how un-prepared for it you were. Suddenly, at the final examination hour's stroke and the intonation 'Put down your pens and hand in your papers' it was all over for good or ill. After the celebration, the Class of '64 hung around College for a few days, nursing their hangovers and comparing their answers to various examination questions with those of others and discovering, disconcertingly, that they were often different, until even this palled and there was nothing left to do. One by one, the class drifted off home, back to their towns of origin to fret on their result. It was still officially term time, so the CEGB made no demands on my time until September and I went back to Manchester, Annie and Julie, exhausted and fretting with the rest of the class. Preliminary and unofficial results were out in late July and time seemed to drag interminably. On results day, Annie and I took Julie to Blackpool, the first family break we had ever had which was great even though it was just a day trip. In the afternoon I found a public telephone box and called the College and Head of Department. After some prevarication, stressing that the result he was about to give me was 'preliminary' and 'unofficial', he finally said the magic words: 'David, the College will award you a First Class Honours. The external assessors have to verify it but I don't expect the official result to be any different. Congratulations.' I felt so elated I ran, clicking my heels as I went, down to the beach where Annie and Julie were building sand castles and shouted the news to Annie. 'I knew you would do it,' she said matter-of-factly. 'Besides, all of the Newton Heath Catholics prayed for it and lit candles.'

Silly me! What could have possibly gone wrong then, I thought.

With the joy and relief came the freedom to put the finishing touches to our upcoming marriage in August and our new life. Life felt very, very sweet.

CHAPTER 9

Mr and Mrs D. C. Fanthorpe

The Irish don't know what they want
and are prepared to fight to the death to get it.

Sidney Littlewood

WE GOT MARRIED ON 15 August 1964 at Christ the King Church, Newton Heath, Father Diggins officiating. It was a great day and a happy and convivial reception at the Bay Horse Inn, Clayton Bridge. My lot had come over from Doncaster in a hired minibus and Annie's lot had gathered from the immediate locality. My Mam and Dad, though disapproving at first, had been won over by Annie in the intervening years since we had first met. In fact Mam told me that if we ever split up, Annie would be welcome in her house, but I would not. Father had generously overcome his aversion to the Catholic Church and at least appeared happy to see his son marry the girl of his choice at last, even with the dubious benefit of Catholic clergy. Apart from an attack of angina half way through the service, his Protestant God made no other comment on his betrayal.

Apart from Father's angina attack, the day went off without a hitch, which, given the planning mayhem that had proceeded it, was a minor Catholic miracle in itself. The planning had been chaotic to say the least. We had decided early that given all the circumstances, we would finance the wedding ourselves. I certainly didn't feel like asking my Mam and Dad for help, and Annie felt the same of hers, so we saved up in a Post Office account every penny we could spare. In the end we had the princely sum of £45 to invest in the great day. Amazingly, this just about covered all the usual affectations of a wedding day: the bride's dress, the cars, the flowers, the church, the photographer and even the wedding reception buffet.

But finance was easy when compared to family logistics and politics. We had planned it so that Annie would leave for the Church from her mother's house, where she would spend the wedding eve, this for propriety's sake. I would leave from our Newton Heath hovel and the cars had been organised accordingly. But in the months proceeding our great day a fearful row had erupted between Annie's mother and father over something that had happened many, many years before, and John Patrick, Annie's father, had sensibly opted for a safe distance and was lost to MacAlpine's Fusiliers somewhere in the wilds of Cumberland mending roads. No one knew of his whereabouts. This was not entirely unusual. Annie's mother Molly had a fearsome temper and a vicious disposition when the past was resurrected, as only an Irishwoman can have, and after witnessing some of these eruptions I could well understand how the Irish were still fighting the 1690 Battle of the Boyne today. I had once unintentionally entered into one of these ferocious arguments. I had called in to see John Patrick and Molly on my way back from the market one Saturday morning, as was my custom. A terrible row was raging about something that had happened some twenty years previously as far as I could gather. I tried to mediate in this and said something like:

'Na then you two, all this was twenty bloody years ago! Surely tha' doesn't need to be fighting o'er it now.'

Bloody hell! John Patrick's unconscious and ancient sins against marriage were instantly put on one side and I became the object of Molly's fury as she turned her fulsome Irish vitriol on me. I retreated suitably chastised with Molly telling me in no uncertain terms it was none of my business and waving a carving knife under my nose to subtly emphasise her point. No, I could well understand John Patrick's strategic absence if it had been one of those tirades.

So as our wedding day approached, John Patrick could not be found, which made Annie very sad, but there was nothing we could do. Then just a few nights before our day, there came a surreptitious knock on our hovel door. I thought it was Molly returning for something she had forgotten because she had been in our house for the last few hours and had only just left. But no, it was John Patrick.

'You've just missed Mam,' said Annie after a tearful reunion.

'I know,' said John Patrick, 'I was waiting for her to leave!'

Annie was delighted that her father had returned to give her away on her big day, but not surprisingly, John Patrick was reluctant to announce his return to Molly in person, so he stayed with us. It was left to Annie to tell her mother of John Patrick's demob from MacAlpine's Fusiliers and that he would be giving her away after all. Well, if John Patrick was going to the wedding, then she most certainly was not, said Molly, and what's more, Annie needn't bother leaving from her house!

I tried and Annie tried, but Molly was implacable, she was not coming to any wedding where John Patrick was going to be and that was that.

Reluctantly, Annie arranged to stay at her bridesmaid's house on her wedding's eve and the cars were reorganised accordingly.

One day before the wedding, a tearful and distraught Molly harangued Annie with her shame at 'my daughter not even leaving her mother's home to go to her wedding. What will the neighbourhood say?'

The fact that she was the cause of this particular shame was lost on Molly and it had suddenly become all Annie's fault.

Patiently, Annie organised a wedding outfit and hairdo for her mother and changed the cars yet again. She would now leave from her mother's house, and both parents would be there. And so it was. If you look at the wedding photographs, all is sweetness and light in the Doherty camp; there is even the hint of a smile on that implacable and fearsome Galway visage.

If ever there was a defining moment that saw an end to childhood and the beginning of adulthood, this was it. It had been a great and rumbustious childhood, an adventurous and sometimes exciting childhood and a life forming childhood, a childhood I could happily wish on others. But now I felt for the first time the true adult weight of responsibility for a wife, a family and a career to go and make. For all that, it really was a great day.

BOOK II

Farewell to Yorkshire

CHAPTER 1

Mega best quality blue

Electricity originates inside clouds. There, it forms into
lightning, which is attracted to the Earth by golfers. After
entering the ground, the electricity hardens into coal,
which, when dug up by power companies and burned in
big ovens called 'generators', turns back into electricity
where it is transformed by TV sets into commercials for
beer, which passes through the consumers and back into the
ground, thus completing what is known as a 'circuit'.

Dave Barry

AFTER OUR WEDDING IN August I began to receive offers of
employment in the Yorkshire region of the CEGB. By far the
most exciting was an offer of a job in the new Thorpe Marsh Power
Station just outside Doncaster. When commissioned this was to be a
mega structure, a monolith of a power station, the size of which took
the breath away. One set alone was to be nearly five times the size of
the whole of Mexborough put together. It was to be the prototype for
a new generation of stations that would henceforth litter the landscapes
of the Yorkshire, Nottinghamshire and Lancashire coalfields, and this
would put me in on the ground floor. The new Superintendent was ex
Mexborough, the very same one I had 'failed to show respect for'
according to the miserable old Scot Charge Engineer back at
Mexborough. The Super obviously never felt the same offence,
because the offer came from him direct. The job had one other major
attraction. There were new council houses available for Thorpe Marsh
employees in the little village of Kirk Sandal. This would solve the
pressing problem of living in the Hovel whose coat of Woolworth's
paint was wearing thin and the remaining structural strength with it.
Having wantonly spent all our life's savings on our big day we hadn't a
penny to our name, so there wasn't really an alternative.

I eagerly accepted the offer and started work at Thorpe Marsh in
September 1964 as a General Assistant Engineer for the unbelievable
consideration of £915 per year. We took one of the council houses
and moved, lock, stock and mangle, to Kirk Sandal, riding with the

removal van driver in his cab all the way from Manchester to Doncaster because we hadn't any money for fares.

There was just one snag to my new appointment. As an apprentice I had been paid weekly. The new job was 'on staff' with the coveted white overalls and paid monthly so in theory I would have to wait one month before I got any pay. Annie had packed in her job to move and we had nothing. The station clerk was very sympathetic and I was given an advance month's pay two weeks before it was due. But this was only postponing the evil day when we would have to live off my monthly salary. By December we had managed somehow, but Christmas loomed. The CEGB came up trumps again and paid us all on Christmas Eve instead of 31 December. We put aside money for rent, rates, coal, electricity and gas and bought Julie a Christmas present of a golliwog together with some food for Christmas Day itself. We were left with £5 to survive on until 31 January. God bless Annie. She made not a word of complaint and invested our £5 in a whole sack of potatoes and a whole carton of dried chicken noodle soup. We ate this in various combinations until the end of January:

> Mashed potatoes with chicken noodle gravy.
> Whole boiled potatoes with chicken noodle gravy.
> Potato and chicken noodle casserole.
> Baked potatoes with a chicken noodle soup starter.
> Pomme de terre avec poulet casserole.
> Pomme de terre à la Concannon avec sauce de poulet.
> Pomme de terre à la champ avec poulet en jus.
> Pomme de bloody terre-ible!

The combinations grew ever more creative. Only an Irishwoman could wreak so much creativity out of potatoes. Having no money to buy lunch in the canteen, I worked through lunch each day so by the time I came home I was famished and fantasising how chicken noodle would be combined with potato today.

The house was new and by the standards of the day quite advanced. It had a kitchen/diner and a lounge and was 'background centrally heated', i.e. it had a radiator in the hall fed from the back boiler in the kitchen. The downstairs was Marley tiled throughout which helped disguise the fact that we had no floor coverings save an old and battered carpet square which went into the lounge as an overgrown rug. But the stairs and bedrooms were wooden floored and because we couldn't afford carpets, they were bare. The house echoed to our every footstep but it was a stately home compared to the Newton Heath hovel.

Thorpe Marsh was a wondrous place in 1964. Mighty cross compounded turbine/alternator sets and boilers the size and scale of cathedrals. I loved it, faults and all. And it had faults. Because this was beyond the scale of anything yet built anywhere in the world and because it was a prototype station it had all sorts of idiosyncrasies. Cross compounding or two separate turbine shafts in one set was a reluctant expediency because they couldn't get anything bigger than half a 550 MW alternator into the site they had chosen outside the little village of Barnby Dun. The two sets that comprised the station were of different make and configuration, likewise the two boilers, this so the CEGB could experiment a little and ultimately decide the best suppliers. It was like learning two different power stations. And whoever had designed the thing had got a few calculations seriously wrong. When trying to fire up the boiler for the first time on auxiliary fuel oil burners, they made almost no headway against the massive thermal inertia of the boiler brutes.

'Like farting in a cathedral with a lighted match. All noise and no heat,' said the Operations Superintendent, a man of few but colourful words.

Eventually after futile days of this, the Operations Superintendent fired up the coal burners and brought the reluctant monster up to temperature and pressure, ever fearful that the rate of temperature increase was now too rapid for the expanding boiler steelwork.

But the technology was amazing for 1964. Because of the scale, everything was automated and instrumentation telemetered back to a central control room. In theory you could actually run this whole gargantuan set-up from the central control room with the help of a few auxiliary plant attendants who scurried about, ant like and largely lost for whole shifts on end in the cathedral of pipes, steel and mega structures.

I absolutely loved it. I was assigned to the Efficiency Department, which in the Yorkshire Region was one man and a dog. Woof!

Actually it was one man and two dogs, both in the form of General Assistant Engineers, the Yorkshire Region never quite having real enthusiasm for squeezing the last calorie out of fuel when they were literally sat on the biggest coal reserves in Great Britain. We were mostly given the task of technical investigation when there was a problem, which was every hour of every day during commissioning, so we were very busy. But the task sent me into every nook and cranny of this technological marvel, measuring, assessing and coming up with solutions. I couldn't have been happier in any other role. This was a technologist's dream come true, a massive, multi million pound Meccano set that I played with for hours, days, even months on end.

After nine months or so, the Efficiency Engineer got promoted elsewhere and I got the job. My pay shot up to £1,700 a year, almost double what I had been on, and Annie and I were confident enough to start making investments in our home. I went to my bank and asked to see the Manager.

'And what is your business with the Manager?' asked the counter clerk.

'I'd like to apply for a bank loan. I'm newly married and I want to buy some furniture,' I replied as if this was the most natural thing in the world.

'I'm afraid the Manager is unavailable for such things. In any case, it is out of the question,' said the counter clerk with such an air of disdain and dismissive finality that I gave up, crushed by his obvious superiority in matters fiscal.

So hire purchase it was. We started with a new bed. The old one, late of the Newton Heath hovel, was a wire mesh support type with an unsprung feather mattress on top, all of which was so high Annie had to take a run at it to get in at all. Unfortunately, the supporting mesh had a large hole in it which the feather mattress and your backside disappeared into if you were foolish enough to lie in the centre of the bed, so you were forced to sleep on one side or the other. A new bed was definitely a first priority even if hire purchase was required. We also invested in linoleum for Julie's and the spare bedroom and a remnant of carpet for the stairs. This was living in style! The promotion couldn't have come at a better time. Annie was pregnant with our second child and nest building was overdue.

David was born in August 1965. It was a remarkably uncomplicated birth at home, though the medical profession tried their hardest to complicate it in the pre-natal clinics during the months before the birth. The GP practice we were part of had a rule that if you were less than five feet tall, then you would have to go into hospital for the birth and they would not attend. Despite Annie's best stretching efforts, the highest she could muster in the doctor's surgery was four feet, eleven and three-quarters, weighed down as she was by an enormous baby. But arbitrary doctor's rules meant nothing to Annie and she was determined to have her baby at home. As the due date approached she was attended by the midwife who would look after her in the post-natal time. She was a young midwife who lived on our street about fifty yards away and Annie liked her. The due date arrived and still no baby. The midwife told Annie she was going on holiday at the end of the week so she would introduce her replacement before she went. Her replacement turned out to be a great, matronly nurse of the old school who came through the house like a ship in full sail dispensing her wisdom and rules as she went and sending expectant fathers scurrying for cover. Annie took an instant dislike to her and willed her baby to make an appearance before her favourite midwife went on holiday. But babies have a way of deciding for themselves, and this one was quite happy where he was, thank you very much. Annie got more and more desperate as the week wore on. Finally, on Thursday evening, she took castor oil and a hot bath. No-one was getting her into hospital if she could help it. We went to bed about midnight and everything was calm. Then twenty minutes later Annie felt 'strange'. Another five minutes and her waters broke and we hurriedly moved into the prepared spare bedroom, chosen because it had linoleum floor covering where ours had none, and I rushed up the road for the midwife. Her house was in darkness and it took five minutes of knocking to get any response. Finally she reluctantly appeared in curlers and nightdress demanding to know what was up. I told her Annie was in labour.

'How long?' she asked.

'Half an hour,' I replied, 'but her waters have broken.'

'Oh all right, then, I'll be there after I get dressed. I thought it was urgent judging by the furore you were creating,' she said, and I hurried back to Annie.

The baby's head had appeared. Oh bloody hell! What's a husband to do?

I rushed back up the road. The midwife came to the door taking her curlers out and ready to tell the panicking father to bugger off.

'The baby is on the way!' I shouted.

'I know it is, you already told me that!' the midwife replied with more than a tinge of impatience and a disdain for fathers shared by all midwives in those days.

'No, no! The baby's head is out. Come quick!'

My panic spread rapidly across the midwife's face like a contagion and with instructions for me to bring the gas and air, she grabbed her bag and shot off down the street to our house, head half covered in curlers. I dropped the gas and air bottles halfway back and the clang they made hitting the road woke those who weren't already awakened by my panic.

And so David was born. From 'feeling strange' to 'all over' took no more than an hour and our GP, when he finally arrived in the peaceful aftermath, said he had never known such a short and uncomplicated delivery.

'It was easy,' I said.

'You couldn't have got a can of Heinz beans through there,' said the doctor by way of puncturing my complacency. 'It was all down to a remarkable mother.'

How true. But then, he didn't know the greased lightning effects of caster oil and hot baths on this particular remarkable, nine and a half months pregnant mother and she wasn't about to tell him.

Thorpe Marsh staggered on and eventually both sets were commissioned. This was punctuated by a cooling tower collapse at neighbouring Ferrybridge C Power Station in November 1965 when, in winds gusting to 85 m.p.h., three of the eight towers fell down. Since my office was immediately below the east towers at Thorpe Marsh and they were exactly the same design as the Ferrybridge towers, I thought it best to evacuate, at least until the winds died down. It was later shown it was the placement of the towers that had funnelled the wind and since ours had nothing like their configuration, we breathed a huge sigh of relief and got on with the million other problems we had.

In those days mega power stations were being built everywhere, and providing you were prepared to move you could get a new and better job every eighteen months if you wished. And so it was in 1967 I moved to Ratcliffe-on-Soar near Nottingham for a higher grade job in a bigger station. This was the same excitement as before, commissioning four 500 MW sets, but this time good and proven equipment and in the Midlands Region which placed a much higher value on efficiency engineering than the Yorkshire Region. But it meant leaving my homeland Yorkshire. I didn't know it then, but I would never return to work in Yorkshire. It didn't seem to matter at the time; after all, I carried it with me, broad Yorkshire dialect still stubbornly and deliberately in place. It was an affectation and an inverted snobbery which became more and more of a problem, mostly for others who struggled to understand and in any case, it was often despised in management circles. This came to a head in 1969 when I was selected for interview for a Management Development role at Midland Headquarters in Solihull. The Regional Director was determined to develop the best management potential of his operational staff and he created development roles as special assistants reporting directly to him so his wisdom would rub off directly onto them. I was flattered to be included on the shortlist. It offered a fast track career development depending on how you performed in the Director's estimation.

The interview day turned into a disaster. On arrival at reception in Solihull I was given a lengthy report and told I would have half an hour to assimilate it and would then be required to give a verbal five minute summary of its contents at the start of my interview. It was a feasibility report on combined cycle power plant and easy meat for an efficiency engineer and post graduate, but there was a lot to be assimilated in thirty minutes. Nevertheless, by interview time I had the vital details committed to memory in the order of importance so I knew exactly how I would present the verbal report and I was shown into the boardroom. I was astounded. I counted eleven people arranged in a U round the table with the legendary Regional Director at its head. There were station superintendents, station chemists, transmission and protection engineers: in fact senior representatives of every function in the Region. In addition there were the two incumbent Management Development Assistants and the Regional Personnel Officer, an animal never before seen in daylight. After introductions I was asked to begin my verbal report. I hadn't even completed the first sentence when the Director interjected.

'OK. That's fine. Now we would like to each ask you some questions,' he said.

To say I was annoyed was an understatement. I was livid. They had put me through thirty minutes of sweaty, stressful hard work for nothing. And I would have shone in my verbal report.

Containing my anger, I answered their questions which ranged the spectrum of technical issues across their functions. This was home ground. The CEGB was renowned for technical interview questions and there was a vast reservoir of questions shared by all interviewees with their colleagues over the past ten years when they returned from their interviews. There were fashions in the interview questions. With the advent of the mega stations there were new technical issues associated with the high temperatures and pressures and a whole new category of questions had been added to the interviewee library. Some of them were a little esoteric to say the least. Hydrogen embrittlement of furnace tubes, silicon poisoning in steam turbines, vanadium poisoning of superheater tubes in oil fired stations and the effect of sea water on austenitic superheater steels were just some I remember. I was reminded of an old Oxbridge story of the student who when asked, 'What were the causes of the Hundred Years War with particular reference to the geo-political forces in Europe in the Caroline War?' in his final examination paper replied, 'I know nothing of these things but here is a picture of King Henry on his white horse.'

Such was the nature of almost any CEGB interview but so far as I recall, I coped with the range they threw at me.

Eventually, the Director called a halt to this and directed his own questions to me.

'How do you see your career developing from here?' he asked.

I told them that by now I thought I was technically proficient but that up to now I had only managed technology and machines, give or take a few General Assistant Engineer dogsbodies and a Grade 10. I needed wider management and in particular man management experience. He nodded agreement.

'So how do you expect to get that after this posting?' he said.

I told them that after a posting at the Midlands Region working directly for him I felt a posting in a smaller power station as a Deputy Superintendent would seem appropriate.

The whole of the smug inquisitors erupted in hearty, uncontrolled laughter. The Director called the panel back to order, saying,

'No, seriously, what do you think should be the next move after this?'

If I had been livid at the start of the interview I was now dangerously incandescent. I told them I was serious and if they weren't then we had probably been wasting each other's time. The

Director didn't take kindly to my truculence and told me my expectations were totally unrealistic, and:

'Besides which your accent is very broad. I think many people would struggle to understand you at all. You must have heard Mr Smith [one of the smarmy incumbents] and his public school accent. What do you think of it?'

I told them that Mr Smith couldn't help his appalling accent; he just hadn't been born with my geographic advantages. The meeting suddenly turned very, very cold but I was told he 'would find something for me at Regional Headquarters' and I left for home. My first intimate encounter with senior management had not gone too well.

I returned to Ratcliffe restless and smarting. In truth I had been growing restless and dissatisfied for some time. The job was extremely enjoyable, and I worked in a great team but it was as I had said, the management of technology. Management science in its wider context was much talked and written about in Britain at that time and Harvard Business School was getting a wide hearing for its revolutionary management papers and its crisp scientific treatment of a wide range of management issues. Even after I had finished my degree at Bradford I had thought fleetingly of staying on and doing a Masters in Business Administration but finances and the sheer impracticality forbade it and I had forgotten all about it. Probably a good decision; many years later I read one of the most influential books on Management I ever found, though I doubt anyone else would recognise it as such at the time. It was *Up the Organisation* by Robert Townsend, a successful Chairman credited with turning round the Avis Car Hire Company in the 60s. Here is what he had to say about Harvard Business School and Business Schools in general in his book:

Don't hire Harvard Business School Graduates. This worthy enterprise confesses that it trains its students for only three posts – executive vice-president, president, and board chairman. The faculty does not blush when HBS is called the West Point of capitalism.

By design, the 'B-School' trains a senior officer class, the non playing *Captains of Industry* [my italics]. People who, upon graduating, are given a whirlwind tour of their chosen company and a secretary and some work to do while they wait for one of the top three slots to open up.

This elite, in my opinion, is missing some pretty fundamental requirements for success: humility; respect for people on the firing line; deep understanding

of the nature of the business and the kind of people who can enjoy
themselves making it prosper; respect from way down the line; a demonstrated record of guts, industry, loyalty down, judgement, fairness and
honesty under pressure.

Robert Townsend: 'Up the Organisation', 1970

Yes, yes, Robert. But apart from that Harvard is OK, right?

But still, I had this itch to get involved in management proper. In
a way, the CEGB fuelled the itch. The Regional Director, in his zeal
to improve management in his organisation, had insisted we all
attended a day's course in 'Management by Objectives'. This turned
out to be a Management Consultancy sales package that parcelled up
the management of a business by using objectives in a pseudo
scientific formulaic method to measure performance. Nevertheless, I
was impressed. It's a measure of my management naivety that this was
all new to me. Only in later years did I recognise the absurdity of the
pseudo scientific approach and that if you weren't managing with
objectives, what the hell were you doing? But the first exposure to
management science intrigued me and I was hooked.

As weeks turned into months and I still hadn't heard from
Regional Headquarters, the itch became unbearable and I started
looking around. I decided an American company would offer the best
management experience, they had a reputation for it, and British
industry at the time was renowned for appalling management, or so
the common view had it. There was still the matter of my
indecipherable accent. It was after all only an affectation retained
purely for effect from a proud Yorkshire heritage. It had to go and I
stopped using its extremes. It was an increasingly forced affectation
and an inverted snobbery anyway, so it took no great effort to drop it.
What was left was OK by me and if others didn't like it that was their
misfortune. Besides which, intelligible regional accents were becoming fashionable with the advent of novels such as *Saturday Night and
Sunday Morning, A Kind of Loving* and *This Sporting Life* in the early
sixties and even the BBC had shifted toward regional accents.

My boss, the efficiency engineer, knew of my restlessness and told
me he was leaving in two months when the job would be mine. But
such was my compulsion by then that even the prospect of his job
couldn't deflect me. I was going in search of 'management' and that
was that.

CHAPTER 2

The Wingfoot Clan

It was wonderful to find America, but it would have been
more wonderful to miss it.

Mark Twain

I WAS EVENTUALLY INTERVIEWED AT THE American Goodyear Tyre
and Rubber Company, the employees of which were known as
'The Wingfoot Clan' after their company logo designed around the
winged foot of Hermes, the mythological Greek God of boundaries
and of the travellers who cross them, of shepherds and cowherds, of
orators and wit, of literature and poets, of athletics, of weights and
measures, of invention, of commerce in general, and interestingly, of
the cunning of thieves and liars. I never did figure out which part of
Hermes's remit they were invoking in adopting Hermes's foot as
their logo; it could have been any.

It was the strangest interview I had ever experienced, not really
surprising since it was my first outside the electricity supply industry.
The Chief Engineer told me he wouldn't be asking technical
questions since I was more qualified than him in my field, but what
was my taste in music? King Henry's white horse sprang to mind
again. I really didn't see the relevance but after an hour of pleasant
chat in this vein he pronounced himself satisfied and offered me the
job. How much was I looking for? I had thought about this before
going to the interview and told him firmly £3,500 pa. He thought
about this for a second then said,

'Are you sure?'

I was adamant this salary was required, but still he persisted.

'Are you sure you wouldn't like to think about it?' he said.

The more he persisted, the more I dug my heels in and so the deal
was done. Poor sap me! He had been trying to tell me gently that he
was willing to offer a lot more but I had misinterpreted his intent and
thought he was trying to talk me down. I had an awful lot to learn
about negotiation.

We moved to Wolverhampton in 1970 and I started work in
Goodyear on 1 April. How very appropriate. It was a busy office

107

with a very big project in prospect, converting the boiler house to natural gas from coal and totally replacing the aged boilers (vintage 1927. If there is one thing I eventually learned about American management it was that they were superb at flogging an asset to death). All very interesting but the management was simply appalling, though with my naivety I was hardly in a position to judge until much later. The Chief Engineer, a really nice man who had recently recovered from a heart attack, was bullied unmercifully by the American Production Director whom he reported to. In addition Engineering was at war with Production who blamed all their shortcomings on the equipment that Engineering provided or maintained while Engineering blamed the Luddite production staff for the deficiencies. Meanwhile all major decisions, including union negotiations, had to be referred to headquarters in Akron, Ohio which made for lengthy planning blight windows and uncertain outcomes. Er, this is not how Harvard Business School painted it, I thought. One comic manifestation of the management inadequacies came at the end of the month when my pay was due. I was called into the Chief Engineer's office and ushered into a far corner out of sight of his door window. There I was surreptitiously given a brown envelope that contained my pay slip and instructed that under no circumstances was I to display the brown envelope to anybody in the office. Apparently the brown envelope conferred some senior staff status that was the envy of all and there would be anger and jealousy if the natives knew. The sheer management cowardice of this would have been hilarious if it hadn't been so pathetic. In any case, we were entitled to eat in the 'Directors' Canteen', which rather gave the game away. So this was American management!

But the work was interesting and wide in variety and there were a few good engineers, but a lot of time-serving jobs worthies. There were two other newcomers, all of us out of the electricity supply industry where Goodyear had been on a recruiting campaign. One in particular headed up the Utilities section, a remarkable young Charge Engineer from the Midlands region, another David. He was widely experienced in utilities; as well he might be having served as a Charge Engineer, and a lot more streetwise than me. I instinctively liked him and Annie and I formed a friendship with Dave and his wife Lottie that lasts to this day. They were the best things to come out of my experience in Goodyear.

The friendship was furthered by a trip to headquarters in Akron, Ohio, undertaken by Dave and myself to introduce us to the senior management over there and to familiarise ourselves with Headquarter operations. My very first trip to the legendary, the almost mythical America! – in fact, my first trip outside the UK.

We arrived in a snowstorm, this being February, and found our hotel. We were hungry and decide to eat out so we asked the receptionist for a recommendation. He gave us one and we enquired whether it was within walking distance. He told us on no account should we walk as the streets were dangerous. Always use the house phone connected directly to a reputable taxi company, he instructed. Somewhat dismayed and disbelieving we nevertheless did as we were told.

We had a very fancy meal and enjoyed it even though the American cuisine was strange to British tastes (a massive seafood medley topped with ice-cream and accompanied by sweet red wine. The strange mixture was only bettered by a breakfast Dave had on his way down to Fayetteville in Carolina when the airline served fried eggs with maple syrup. Dave was not best pleased) and eventually we were replete and tired so we enquired of the head waiter about a taxi.

'Did you ask for your driver to come back, Sir?' he enquired.

We answered 'No' and he gave us bad news.

'Taxi drivers will not come out to pick up strangers. Too dangerous, Sir,' he said.

We eventually persuaded him to call the taxi company and tell them there were two harmless, innocuous, even saintly, Limeys stranded without their help, and, much to our relief, they turned up. The American Dream I had harboured for so long wasn't supposed to be like this.

Next morning I found a table for breakfast in the pleasant glass fronted restaurant with views of the street outside. A clock tower opposite had today's temperature displayed high so everyone could see it — $17°F$ it said. That's bloody cold beyond my experience, I thought. The waitress appeared and unbidden, poured me a glass of ice-water, ice cubes tinkling in the glass as she poured. Minus $17°$ outside and I get ice-water for breakfast? Altogether a very strange place, America, I concluded.

Eventually a lugubrious headquarters manager turned up to ferry us into the office, complaining bitterly of the vandalising of funeral parlours by modern development in Akron in answer to our questions about the city. By now I had decided that America and Americans were not just strange, they were quite mad.

The headquarters were big. During the tour our guide took us through the main office, a vast open-plan area the size of several football pitches, desks in neat innumerable rows lit by harsh fluorescent lights. At the desks sat the headquarters staff, row upon row of white, shining faces bent over their desks working assiduously to a man. Suddenly, among the sea of white faces, there was a black face.

'That's our conscience nigger,' said our tour guide as we passed.

The poor guy must have felt like he was in the Ku Klux Klan rather than the Wingfoot Clan. Welcome to America 1970, affirmative action, ice-water, sugar dependency, street anarchy and all.

Some time after our return from America, the loud Production Director called me into his office. He told me the electrical staff engineer had resigned in their Northern Ireland plant and he wanted me to go over and stand in. I told him I was happy doing what I was doing and in any case, though I was an academic electrical engineer, I had never practised it.

'Ya frightened of it?' he bellowed by way of question or statement, I wasn't quite sure which.

I told him firmly and with conviction that I was frightened of nothing in engineering, but he had a right to know I was not a practising electrical engineer. I would do it if he and the Chief Engineer wanted me to. The timid Chief Engineer sniggered at my effrontery with the Production Director and each said they were in a tight corner and they wanted me to go. Fine, I said, and I was commissioned to go the following week.

Northern Ireland was a troubled land in 1970. The sectarian divide had re-asserted itself and Catholic civil rights were being campaigned vigorously. When I arrived at the office the Assistant Staff Engineer, after introductions, surreptitiously enquired whether I kicked with my left or right foot. I thought it a strange question and told him I hadn't played football for years lest he was trying to enrol me in the factory football team. He laughed uproariously and said,

'No, no! I meant are you a Proddy or a Teague?'

I told him I was a Prod and he relaxed. From then on we got along famously. Comfortably married to a 'Teague' and instructed in their faith, I really struggled to understand the great Northern Ireland divide but I still think that was to my credit.

I had brought my car over on the Heysham/Belfast ferry because the Company wouldn't run to a hire car, and I got the first intimation of 'the troubles' as a result. Flying home for the weekend, Security told me to be sure and park my car right up behind the gatehouse.

'What for?' I enquired.

'Because with the English plates, the feckin' Teagues will take it for a car bomb if we can't keep an eye on it,' he replied.

Hmm. Very reassuring.

The weeks went by and eventually, after the Irish Plant Chief Engineer had had a good look at me, they offered me the job on a permanent basis, which, I suppose, had always been their plan. I refused point blank on the basis that I could not bring my family to live over there. Just the weekend previously I had flown home as usual. Ulster Bank had built a prefabricated branch right outside our factory gates to service our factory and the burgeoning industrial estate round us. When I returned on Monday, the Bank had gone, blown to smithereens by the IRA, though the concrete base and strongroom bolted securely to it remained. Not a good time to ask me to relocate with a young family in a mixed faith marriage. Catholic women who consorted with Protestants had been known to be tarred and feathered in the Land of Saints and Scholars. So they recruited a native and I stood in until the new man arrived. I left the troubled and tragic land with my car still intact and with few regrets. Things would only get worse for them from then on.

CHAPTER 3

The Glasgow kiss

The great thing about Glasgow is that if there's a nuclear
attack it'll look exactly the same afterwards.

Billy Connolly

EVENTUALLY, IN JUNE 1971, they made me another offer I couldn't
refuse. The Plant Engineering Manager had resigned at their
Scottish plant in Glasgow or had been pushed, I never knew which.
Go and stand in, I was told. This time there were no arguments since
this would get me real management experience and I started many
months of a long commute from Wolverhampton to Glasgow early
every Monday morning, not returning until Friday night each week.
Annie, as usual, was left to run the house and cope with all the family
problems that arose, which she did with aplomb and few complaints.
Good lass, Annie!

How does one begin to describe the awfulness of that Goodyear
Scottish plant in 1971? It was located to the west of Glasgow on the
Great Western Road and between the people's republican anarchy of
Clydebank and Drumchapel, a lawless 'scheme' or sink estate
populated by feckless Rab C. Nesbitt look- and act-alikes. The
labour was all ex-Clydebank Shipyard and as the Scottish Personnel
Assistant said, his job was to give the company away to them as
slowly as possible. They were an unmanageable, anarchic rabble who
had more enthusiasm for the class war than for addressing the tyre
industry competition. In my first week there, the Union shop steward
sidled up to me as I was coming into the factory, and this scion of
the working and downtrodden classes everywhere, this champion of
the Internationale, warned me not to bring a load of 'they darkies'
up there to undercut the local workers, a reference to the high
number of Asians working in the Wolverhampton plant. Apparently
they thought the appointment of an Englishman (well, a Yorkshire
man anyway) was a precursor to an Asian invasion, such was their
Trotskyish paranoia. Welcome to the land of the noble working class
heroes created by Jimmy Reid in his famous Upper Clyde Shipyard
'work in'. Jimmy famously addressed the workers at the yards where

112

he instructed them that there should be 'no hooliganism, no vandalism and no bevvying [drinking]'. If only! That 'work in' in 1971 must have been the most novel experience the shipyard workers and the Govan management ever had.

To run the plant, Goodyear, in its wisdom, had sent an American general manager whose last posting had been on the Asian rubber plantations. I suppose they thought that if he could survive the head hunters of Borneo, he might survive the Clydebank natives. He was amply aided and abetted by an American personnel manager who had been promoted to the post out of the Akron plant because he was an over-able shop steward there and a thorn in their side. Ah well, if you can't beat them, join them.

Drinking was a constant problem. Once, a delivery driver carrying a mixed load including whisky from a nearby distillery was foolish enough to open his rear doors before reversing onto the loading dock. In the time it took him to reverse the lorry onto the dock, his whisky consignment had disappeared as if by magic. The next morning there was pandemonium. The afternoon shift had got roaring drunk on their whisky windfall and had to be sent home incapable. The morning saw the bloody aftermath when disciplinary action had to be contemplated, not an easy matter with the Clydebank crew.

Even my own professional staff was not immune from the drinking problem. One of my mechanical engineers had gone out to visit suppliers and was due back in the afternoon. He didn't turn up and I needed him so I got his assistant to ring round the suppliers to find him. He wasn't there and he couldn't be found. That evening at home I got a call from the missing engineer, blind drunk and screaming obscenities at being 'harassed' by following phone calls all day. I put the phone down on him, livid with rage myself at his obscene phone invasion of my home.

The annual shutdown when the whole of Glasgow is off work and 'doon the watter' was the prime maintenance period when we could get at the machinery without interference from the Luddite mob. My first shutdown turned into an unmitigated disaster. The one Callender machine (vital in tyre manufacture) the plant possessed was to have its rollers replaced and a vital but leaky concrete hot water sump was to be demolished and replaced by a steel tank. All the rest of the equipment was to get routine annual maintenance. I had planned it meticulously in the short time available, with fitters assigned to the various jobs and an inventory of spares taken to make sure the parts were there. After the first week the entire factory was lying in pieces ready for parts replacement and maintenance. Scary with the Luddite mob due back in three weeks, but all planned. Then a series of disasters struck, one after the other, that even to this day I shudder at. The first was an approach by one of the fitters, ominously accompanied by the poisonous shop steward, for an advance on his pay. Apparently he had taken his holiday pay the Friday before and enjoyed a riotous weekend of drinking and carousing until his entire holiday pay had gone. He wasn't due any more pay until after the shutdown when he would get the lieu and overtime pay. I had to tell him 'No' after taking advice from the Personnel Department in Wolverhampton. Advances weren't in the union agreement. In that case, said the shop steward, they would all go on strike. No amount of pleas to the Personnel Department

Personnel (People vs.): Fire the whole personnel department.
                              Robert Townsend, 'Up the Organisation', 1970

to temper the policy would persuade them to change their mind, and the shop steward was adamant. After losing three precious days of the shutdown arguing back and forth, I gave the carouser a personal loan to tide him over and the shop steward reluctantly agreed to withdraw his threat. While this was going on I got my second blow. The new Callender machine rollers had been fitted still with their grease and paper protection. When the paper and grease was cleaned off it revealed the surface of the rollers pitted and corroded up to a millimetre deep. The grease had degenerated over the many years' storage and corroded the surface. They were totally useless. Ah well, we'll just refit the old ones, I said. But no, with totally isolated efficiency the old ones had been sent to the scrapyard as soon as they were removed. There was probably a scam in there somewhere.

In quick succession, the third blow struck. The contractors who had been busy demolishing the old concrete hot water sump (or so I thought) threw in the towel. They were making almost no impression on the old tank with their pneumatic drills. They had done enough however to make it totally unusable. So two of the prime pieces of equipment required for the plant to run at all were unusable and there were no prospects of them recovering by the end of the shutdown and at that stage the entire maintenance crew were going on strike. Yes, yes, but *apart* from that, I hear you say.

We eventually got the plant back to work several weeks after the end of the shutdown after many failed 'solutions' to our problems:

'What do you mean, linish it?'

'I mean grind away the surface using a linishing machine.'

'THA' WHAT? [remember? 'I am incredulous and I don't believe what you are saying'] You want to sandpaper the thing smooth? YOU WANT TO REMOVE ONE MILLIMETRE OF CARBON STEEL ACROSS A SIX FOOT ROLLER WITH A BLOODY BELT SANDER? Bugger off and don't be so daft!'

or

The factory insurer: 'Let me get this right. You want to blow up a concrete tank with dynamite in the middle of a factory surrounded by a housing estate? Yes, I know it's only Drumchapel and I take it on advisement that a bloody good explosion would actually improve it, but even so . . .'

Nevertheless, that's exactly what we did. Sadly, Drumchapel survived unscathed.

It wasn't all disaster, doom and gloom though. The other managers, who had drink demons of their own, quickly latched on to the fact that I was staying in a hotel, and a hotel resident had the power to entertain his guests long after the normal pubs closed in a strictly enforced licensing regime in Scotland at the time. This meant they invited themselves to be my guests many evenings straight after work when they would drink until two in the morning or whenever Morag the barmaid ran out of patience and closed the bar, whichever came soonest. How they managed this with their wives I never knew. I suppose the wives were conditioned to Scottish husbands and their drinking proclivities; either that or they were glad of the peace in the house. They had several frights though. One night, way after midnight, the noisy alcohol-fuelled patter was suddenly and rudely silenced as two of Glasgow's finest walked through the door. Great hulking policemen with broken noses and cauliflower ears, testament to years of duty on Glasgow's mean streets, they surveyed the suddenly silenced room severely for a full twenty seconds for effect, then taking his cap off and hurling it unerringly across the room to land expertly on an empty pint mug their leader said, 'Right! Who's buying?' There was a huge sigh of collective relief from the 'bona fide travellers' and erstwhile managers and the party picked up where it left off, the polis happily whiling away their nightshift with half pints of lager and half drams of whisky, a 'ha'f an' a ha'f' as the Glaswegians so elegantly put it, and the managers not yet ready to contemplate how they would placate wives bearing burnt dinners.

Then there was the American Personnel Manager. One early morning, weaving his way inexpertly home after a long session at the hotel, he was stopped by the police, who correctly identified the fact that he had driven a temporary red light at some roadworks some mile back down the road.

'They couldn't fool me though,' said the Personnel Manager. 'I knew there were no roadworks. They were just trying to trap me.'

Amazingly, the police had vindicated his raddled judgement and let him drive home.

'They Yanks are mair bother than they're worth. There's nae traffic aboot. Let the lard arsed bas' gae.'

'But he's steaming!'

'Aye, but afore ye know it he'll want the American Consul, a public defender and a phone call. Nay, we dinna want to spend the rest of the shift processing him, let the bawbag go.'

'Aye, right.' Then, 'Just be careful how ye' gae Jimmy!'

The hotel barmaid's husband was another great source of after work amusement. He took it on himself to school me in the future City of Culture's attractions. Ibrox Park and a pre-season friendly with Everton was one of the many cultural delights. The two teams were compatible bedfellows, both having Protestant roots in sectarian divided cities. A scruffy urchin of eight or nine approached as I parked the car in a side street.

'Mind your car, mister?' he asked innocently.

'Ye had better pay or there won't be much left of yer car when we come back,' said my mentor.

'Aye, all right. How much?'

'Gi' him a pund. It'll be fine.'

'It's a fiver, mister,' said the cheeky urchin.

'It's a pund an' think yoursel' lucky I dinna burst yer heid,' said my mentor, and the negotiation was complete, as was my car when we returned.

I could hardly believe the match. A pre-season friendly and Ibrox was all but noisily full. Still, it was the English who were up to be taught a lesson even if they had the dubious distinction of being Proddies and 'Flower of Scotland' said it all for them:

> . . . And send them homeward,
> Tae think again.'

The Corries, 'Flower of Scotland'

Football figured large in Glasgow culture and it was my mentor who also took me to the Bankies Club, the 'Social' club of the Clydebank SFC. After a pleasant evening of ha'fs of heavy, whisky chasers and good patter, we were about to leave when, passing through the entrance lobby, we came across a casual altercation between two men, either of whom could have demolished my obstinate concrete tank single handed and without raising a sweat. Suddenly, out of what had been a relatively civilised exchange (well, civilised by Clydebank standards, razors hadn't been drawn yet) one of the men savagely head butted the other whose nose exploded in a shower of blood and snot, and battle-proper commenced. I had never seen a head butt before but I suspected I now knew what 'Burst yer heid' meant.

'Bloody hell! What was that?' I asked my mentor from the safe distance of the car park.

'That, David, was the Glasgae kiss,' he replied.

'Kiss? THAT'S A KISS?'

I still hadn't got the hang of Glasgow's humorous heavy irony. I'd hate to see the full conjugal relationship, I thought and we sped back to the hotel and Morag's relatively civilised and tender ministrations. When we got back to the hotel bar, Morag's father was in. He was an alcoholic and only visited his daughter's bar at the tail-end of a bender, the only times he had the courage to face his Amazonian girl.

'Away fayther, an' gi' me peace afore I burst yer heid!' Morag was bellowing. 'Away hame and drink yer Buckie there, I dinna want you in here. Yer in the electric soup again.'

How such a diminutive little man came to produce such a strapping lassie as Morag is best left to the imagination, but I now knew that Glasgow kissing was not involved. He bowed to her undoubted physical superiority and left.

Ah, the joys of The City of Culture's social scene.

Eventually, I also bowed to the inevitable and moved the family up. I had been commuting from Wolverhampton for nine months now and I was fed up with it. It had cost me a car engine and several near misses on the M6 and A74. Driving up to Glasgow early one Monday morning, I had reached the long drag up the hill outside Ecclefechan, and after some injudicious and impatient acceleration on the steep hill, my engine gave a very large bang followed by an ominous sustained tinkling sound. I got towed into Ecclefechan and the local garage who had the cylinder head off in no time at all. That was the end of rapid reparations. One of the six cylinders was completely empty save for a piston rod that was now flailing about loose and serving only to batter the cylinder walls into submission. A valve had dropped and completely demolished the piston. The tinkling had been the piston fragments falling into the sump, being pulled through the oil pump and distributing themselves without prejudice throughout the remaining five cylinders leaving deep scars in each as they went. Bugger! The garage proprietor said a new engine was required and it would take weeks. I'm not surprised, I thought. Even when they have found a new engine it would take another month to find Ecclefechan. So how to get to Glasgow from Ecclefechan early on a Monday morning? The proprietor was helpful.

'The railway runs through here,' he said and waited for my hopes to rise. My hopes rose.

'But the station closed back in the sixties. You'll ha' to gae back to Carlisle to catch a train.'

'Taxi?' I enquired.

'Carlisle,' he replied.

'Rental car?'

'Carlisle. There is a bus comes through here though. Goes all the way to Glasgow.'

Ah, sense at last.

'What time does it come through?' I asked with relief.

'Thursday,' he replied without a trace of the ridicule he was undoubtedly exercising on the itinerant Sassenach and engine murderer, 'But you can catch one any day in . . .'

'Carlisle,' I interjected wearily.

He mellowed suddenly, probably noting the glint that was rapidly growing in my angry eyes.

'There's a delivery lorry comes through here every Monday though, aboot noon time. He might gae yer a lift if ye ask him nicely.' And so it was.

But finding a house in or around Glasgow was not easy at that time. The prices were rapidly catching up to London and houses sold within days of going to market, sometimes within hours. Eventually I found a repossessed property in the highly desirable Helensburgh, a seaside town about eighteen miles west of Glasgow. Because the bank wanted rid of it, it was reasonably priced. But why had it not gone already? It was a modern four-bedroom detached house, a little eccentric in its design with one bedroom and the bathroom downstairs but otherwise a perfectly nice house. After detailed inspection I thought the answer to that was the state of the garden and the plumbing. The house had stood empty for nine months or more through the winter. The garden was a jungle and all the central heating pipes had burst at the joints. But no big deal for a utilities engineer, I thought. It looked far worse than it was. I went in with my offer the same day and the bank accepted with worrying alacrity. Under Scottish law, the house was now mine. There was no time to consult Annie about the purchase and the first she saw of it was when we pulled up outside, ahead of the removal van by a couple of hours. The car stopped at the kerb and Annie looked at my proud purchase speechless for all of five minutes. Then she cried quietly. And she hadn't even seen the eccentricities and plumbing damage inside. Double bugger! From that discouraging start, we set to and brought the house interior back to its former glory over the next few months. The garden wilderness would have to wait its turn. In any case, from moving in on 18 March 1972, it rained constantly for six weeks. Even the Bible only allowed for forty days and forty nights, but this was the west of Scotland, that you could easily believe was outside the Bible's remit in more ways than one. I was still putting the finishing touches to the garden in November when we decided we had had enough of Goodyear and Scotland, and I sought pastures new.

We had made a lot of good friends in Helensburgh, some of who endure to this day, and friends had come up to see us with their families, always a highlight of our Scottish existence. Dad and Mam also came up, on their railway-issued free passes, so we didn't feel totally cut off. But my problems in the plant were compounded by a whole range of other issues. Son David had settled extremely well in his new primary school, in fact in those few short months he had acquired a Scottish accent and a worrying liking for the kilt, but

daughter Julie had not settled at all in the Academy. She got quite a
bad time from some of the Scottish kids and not the best of treatment
from the teachers either. There was an undercurrent of anti English
sentiment in Helensburgh, as there was in Glasgow, and it surfaced
only too readily. Annie experienced the same thing shopping in the
town. And then there was the Scottish drinking culture. I took Dad
down to the hotel in town for a Sunday lunch pint, as was his
custom. The pubs couldn't open on Sunday under the Scottish
licensing law then but hotels could serve 'bona fide travellers'. With
our English/Yorkshire accents and our strange taste in drinks we
easily passed for bona fide travellers.

'Two pints of bitter, please.'

'Will tha' be the heavy yer asking fer?'

'Ah yes, heavy.'

'Will yer be wanting a ha'f a dram wi' tha'?'

'No, thank you.'

'Please yersel', Jimmy.'

We walked into the bar. Rolling about on the floor were two
women, screaming, spitting and clawing at each other accompanied
by some very ripe language. Nobody in the busy bar took a blind bit
of notice. I stepped over the protagonists and ordered the couple of
pints. Father was bewildered at first. Personally, I was fully ac-
climatised. When there didn't seem to be any prospect of a knockout
or even points verdict and the cat fight continued, Father's Protestant
ethic reasserted itself, and he said, 'Drink up, lad, we're off!' Shame;
I was all for waiting to see whether the fried battered Mars Bar
heavyweight harridan would beat her lightweight opponent or
whether the smaller harridan would prevail. She was obviously a
Proddy from her pinched and mean face, or so the Catholics said. My
money was on the lightweight. This was turning into a marathon and
she was built for endurance. Alas, I would never know.

Then there was Glasgow Fairs weeks when a lot of Glasgow
descended 'doon this particular watter' at Helensburgh. Annie and I
were driving down town in the Fairs and stopped at a traffic light.
When it turned to green, I set off and a passing drunk stepped straight
in front of my bumper. I braked hard and the bumper nudged him
as the car rocked forward.

'See you Jimmy, Yer looking fer a burst heid?' he shouted,
expletives deleted.

Then he set about trying to tip the car over on its roof. His drunken enthusiasm alone was no great concern, but when the passing drunks saw the fun, they joined in too. I eased the car away as gently as possible into the traffic and the drunk fell in the gutter with his car-hurling team mates, smashing his bottle of Buckie in the process. The old music hall song described the scene perfectly as far as I was concerned:

One evening in October,
When I was one-third sober,
An' taking home a 'load' with manly pride;
My poor feet began to stutter,
So I lay down in the gutter,
And a pig came up an' lay down by my side;

Then we sang, 'It's all fair weather
When good fellows get together,'
Till a lady passing by was heard to say:
'You can tell a man who "boozes"
By the company he chooses'
And the pig got up and slowly walked away.

Benjamin Hapgood Burt: 'THE PIG!'

The same evening, we were in the fish and chip shop ('Fried Battered Mars Bars – 20 pence') in a long queue when a man in front of us made some comment about Celtic Football Club, and a man behind us wearing green and white took serious exception to this. It began to develop. Apparently there had been an 'Old Firm' clash that day and at least half of Glasgow didn't like the result. That's the trouble with Celtic/Rangers matches. Worse still, enthusiastic representatives of winners and losers were in the queue and we were sandwiched. I suppose one solution would have been to demonstrate our impeccable English accents, when 'Old Firm' rivalries would have been put on one side, at least for a time, but I didn't fancy that solution much and we slunk out, fish and chip-less but with our teeth intact and our heids un-burst. I decided that the family and my career would be best served by moving back to England and I started looking round.

This time I was a lot more selective and careful. Black and Decker were advertising regularly and they enjoyed a very high management reputation at the time, regularly featured admiringly in *Management Today* and having quite extraordinary results in the marketplace. I went for interview as a Production Engineering Manager for their new plant in County Durham. I knew absolutely nothing about production engineering in manufacturing plants but since when did that put me off anything – it had 'Engineering' in the job title, how difficult could it be? I thought. The interview at their Maidenhead headquarters was good and mutually satisfying, and they asked me to go to their Spennymoor plant for interview by the General Manager up there. That went well too and eventually they said even though they couldn't offer me the Production Engineering Manager job because of my lack of relevant experience, they wanted me on board and would make me an offer in due course. It came within days, Plant Engineering Manager at the princely sum of £4,750 p.a. There was one fatal drawback though. The job I had applied for had the same salary but a company car in addition. This offer had no company car. Disappointed, I wrote back and said, 'No, thank you,' and why. I thought nothing more about it for the next few days until one evening, returning home, Annie told me she had had a wonderful phone call from someone at Black and Decker who, when he discovered I was still at work, proceeded to tell her how much they wanted me to join them and that I should give them another chance to persuade me at a further interview. Annie was very impressed and even charmed by the caller and proceeded to do his job for him in persuading me to go again for interview. What a smoothie he was, as I later discovered after joining. World War II Spitfire Pilot Officer, immaculate accent that would cut glass at thirty paces and very astute and whose sole job really was to garner the best of available management talent for the burgeoning Black and Decker; in fact, their in-house headhunter and king-maker.

So I gave it another go and this time I was interviewed by the Managing Director who was extremely impressive and well worthy, I judged, of the admiring *Management Today* and *Financial Times* articles. He told me that for internal political reasons, he couldn't give me a company car on starting the job, but in lieu of a car, what was it worth to me? I hadn't thought about this possibility, so I did a quick bit of mental arithmetic on the cost of running my car, added a bit and said, '£500 per year.'

'Done,' he said, and before I had time to change my mind he had a contract in front of me with a pen and the deal was done. I handed in my written resignation at Goodyear Glasgow with very bad grace,

something I have regretted since, telling them in no uncertain terms
what I thought about their ramshackle operation. Very bad form.

At the end of my time with Goodyear, three years in all, I had
learned a lot about commercial company ways, man management and
American management in particular, even if the learning was 'how
not to do it'. I had managed to learn something of finance, enrolling
at the Strathclyde University for evening classes for two courses in
financial management during my commuting period and applying it
in managing the departmental budget and capital planning for the
plant. Such learning, and its scars, made me even more determined
and better armed to do it right the next time.

We left Scotland after a riotous Hogmanay with warm memories
if no regrets. Annie had eventually passed her driving test there after
several failed attempts, negotiating the roads round the distillery in
Dumbarton, and I got her her very first car for that leaving
Christmas, so it has always been remembered for that. So much was
thought of Annie's success that our friend Lottie wrote a poem to
celebrate Annie's successful driving test.

Tried and Won

Ann is excited,
Thrilled and delighted,
Her husband relieved,
Approving and pleased.

She has tried and mastered it,
Reversed and three pointed it,
The examiner has passed it,
Her prowess behind the wheel.

Lottie Hollingsworth

And we had new friends who we still keep in touch with today. I
don't know what sort of reputation I left behind me. Certainly my
first shutdown, against which plant engineers are most conspicuously
judged, had been a catalogue of disasters. On the plus side though, I
had eventually managed to imprint a semblance of order and
engineering intellect into what otherwise had been a shambles.
Wolverhampton Headquarters wanted the Glasgow Plant Manager to
persuade me to stay, until they read the resignation letter I had
written. Either in a similar pique to my letter's, or because they
recognised the hopelessness of the cause, they gave up and on

2 January 1973 I set off for a new life in County Durham and Black
and Decker, severely hung-over from Hogmanay, but otherwise
cheerful and hopeful.

CHAPTER 4

. . . if production can keep pace

May: the Marketing Director
Senses he might now detect a
Movement in the market place,
If Production can keep pace.

Bertie Ramsbottom: 'Businessman's Diary'
from The Bottom Line

THEY WERE EXCITING TIMES IN Black and Decker. Their introduction of an electric drill which retailed for £5 in 1964 had
transformed the business. It brought electric tools within reach of the
average Do–It–Yourself–er for the first time. And back then, we were
all Do–It–Yourself–ers from servicing our own cars to painting and
decorating and general house and machinery repair. Few could afford
to do other on the household income of the day. There was no 'Let's
get a man in' then. Cars were only purchased after careful scrutiny of
the ease of self servicing. I had once considered buying a Jaguar Mark
10 at a car auction. It was 'only' £300, immaculate and magnificent.
But one look under the bonnet and I knew that self servicing of this
monster was an impossibility and the tantalising prospect of driving
about in a limousine for £300 melted away like a chocolate teapot
keeping warm on the hob. I bought a Vauxhall Viva in need of a
paint job instead. Jaguars would have to wait.

The new drills had revolutionised DIY retailing and sold in their
thousands. Annie had bought me one for Christmas in 1965 which
is still working today. I was typical of hundreds of thousands of others
as indeed was Annie in her choice of present for her husband, and
for many years Black and Decker solved the perennial wives' problem
of what to buy their husbands for Christmas, birthday, anniversary or
'What a lovely husband you are' day, though the last was much rarer.
All right, it never happened, but you know what I mean. Black and
Decker became the universally acceptable, even coveted, gift to a
man. This too became part of the retail revolution in DIY, the
concept of buying electric tools for annual occasions rather than by
need of job. And this had its consequences for the manufacturer who

had to produce for the peak Christmas gifting season rather than
evenly all year. The DIY retail revolution was epitomised by a Mr
Block and a Mr Quayle who founded a DIY supermarket chain on
the back of it, and B&Q was born.

When I joined in January 1973, the factory had just emerged from
the Christmas blitz and was being re-jigged for the garden season sales
which counterbalanced the power tool sales season. Black and Decker
had been growing at a compound rate of 15 per cent per year since
that drills introduction, a figure only limited by the ability of the
factory to keep pace with demand.

The Spennymoor factory had been built as a result in 1967, so it
was still new when I joined. By power tool manufacturing standards
it was a monster, 50,000 square metres of prime factory floor space,
purpose built, helped by a grateful local authority and development
agency desperate to provide employment opportunities in the
north-east of England which was full of dead and dying industries and
consequently, of the unemployed. Black and Decker manufacturing
had, until then, been in the south of England, in Maidenhead and
Harmondsworth. The company had come north in search of labour,
Heathrow and the burgeoning south-east economy making it almost
impossible to find in the south. When the Chairman had announced
the move to County Durham, the unions quickly latched onto the
fact that the Harmondsworth and Maidenhead factories were non-
unionised and indeed, that Black and Decker were non-union in
principle. This would never do! The capitalist bastards were coming
north to exploit the downtrodden workers, they said loudly, widely
and indignantly with their usual impeccable turn of sophisticated
phrase. They anticipated that Black and Decker would pay a lower,
northern rate of pay rather than the inflated rate it took to find
anybody in London and its surrounds. The Chairman let them build
up a head of steam without comment until this became the burning
issue. He then announced, with a phrase that could have come
straight out of Tony Blair's *Boys' Book of Sound Bites* (although Tony
Blair wasn't invented yet. More of that later. Come to think of it,
sound bites weren't invented yet either) that:

'We are coming to Durham to make money, not save it. Rates of
pay for all grades will be the same north and south.'

That had been the end of that particular debate and the unions
went off to contemplate a longer term strategy of hurling any abuse

that included the words 'Union bashing' or 'Rights' or 'Who can we bring out on strike to make them see sense?' We couldn't have known then, but it was to be an as yet unknown Tony Blair who would finally put an end to the abuse. It's a funny old life.

In January 1973 the factory was a mess. As ever they had been under tremendous stress to produce more than they were able. The assembly shop was a disaster area as the assembly lines for garden product were replacing the power tool lines. There was material everywhere, though plenty of space to put it, and an air of frenzied chaos reigned. The whole thing was presided over by the General Manager, who, it turned out, was an arrogant, bombastic bully. The North-Easterners, whom I quickly warmed to, had named him Genghis with that dry wit that characterises societies used to hardship. I quickly learned he had to be tough though. Given the inadequacy of the inherited systems from much smaller, more mature, plants, the raw labour, the dearth of management talent back in the seventies, and the insatiable demand for yet more production, he was the only thing that held it together at all. Despite the bombast, I liked him. The factory was trying to produce 40,000 power tools a week and try as mightily as the tough and good-hearted Geordies did, it wasn't being achieved. It was the Holy Grail and seemed just as unreachable. This was the scene I had inherited and I joined the frenzy.

Plant engineering had been run by an able and good hearted engineer but who was almost totally devoid of motivation. I quickly learned he was a Jehovah Witness.

'Welcome to Black and Decker, David. Now, have you heard Jehovah's message?'

'Heard it? My Uncle Ted practically invented it,' I told him.

This probably explained his lack of enthusiasm for a manufacturing plant's daily, even hourly, priorities. With the end of the world imminent, since I was three to my certain knowledge, he could hardly be expected to worry too much about today's production, let alone next year's.

As a result Plant Engineering was virgin territory and in that respect it was easy even though the high volume production environment and technologies were alien to me. My Jehovah's assistant just rolled with the punches and shrugged his shoulders. And the punches were coming thick and fast from a desperate production department eager to find scapegoats for production shortfalls in

machine downtime and tardy installation and while Plant Engineering took the flak, all the other departments could relax a little with
such an easy target to soak up the blows. And then there was Genghis
at his weekly Management Operating Committee dishing out the
punishment that multiplied the daily blows twenty-fold. It only took
a month before I decided I wasn't going to take crap like that. I
would hold my hands up to true Plant Engineering responsibility and
put it right but the rest was going to be fired right back with interest.
I quickly made big changes to the departmental structure, motivation
and systems and the boys responded with gusto. They were tired of
the unjustified flak as well. The maintenance crew were good men.
There was the usual mix of experts and heavy mob and some good
foremen. There was one bolshie Glaswegian who bridled at authority, change and anything else he could think of that generally began
with an F, but even he was a damned good tradesman and providing
Celtic won and England kept on losing he got on with his work with
barely audible growls of dissent. I knew Glaswegians by now.

After a couple of months Plant Engineering was no punch bag at
all. Responsibility had been put where it belonged which motivated
the production department to do something about their own
problems and to some extent change targets. When we had genuine
problems with equipment I stood up and told them before they could
tell me and always, always, with a public plan as to what would be
done about it. Genghis himself professed that progress was being
made which was about as triumphantly endorsing as the original
Genghis saying, 'Progress was being made,' after the conquest of India
then Persia and Turkey. He probably did say it, continuing as he did
to conquer Poland, Hungary and half the known world and putting
the fear of God into the remainder.

Two other newcomers had started with me, both, as I recall,
recruited from US operations of General Electric which was greatly
admired at the time, though they were both English. However, one
by one, they fell by the wayside, one after just a few months and the
second by September. On each occasion Genghis and the Personnel
Director sought to reassure me that this wasn't a hire-and-fire
company at heart, but when it was obvious it wasn't going to work
out it was better for everyone that they 'sought to pursue their career
elsewhere' in the time honoured expression. Fair enough, I said, it
was good of them to point this out to me. When the second one

went in September they must have been seriously concerned as to
my confidence in my own future, so much so that they gave me an
embarrassingly good performance review, a big pay rise, a company
car and a promotion. Enough, enough! I'm convinced. I won't be
looking round for opportunities elsewhere, I said. Honest. And I
didn't.

Truth was, I loved it all and the company style in particular. It was
tough hard work and I seldom saw home before 8.00 p.m., but to
counter the immense accountability they placed on you there were
vast freedoms to manage and operate as you thought fit. That was the
essence of their style, high responsibilities and even higher account-
abilities, but providing you lived within your budget (their prime
accountability at the time) and delivered progress then you were left
to get on with it. Easy really. I didn't know at that time why other
companies didn't have the same policy, such was my naivete. I was
learning so much so fast in such a demanding environment and in
such good company that that alone was job satisfaction. However pay
rise, company car and promotion weren't bad either.

By now we had moved the family into County Durham. How we
got there was problematical. The house in Scotland had been sold at a
handsome profit the same day it appeared in the paper, 20 December
1972. As part of the sale agreement we were to vacate at the end of
January. No problem, I thought, our handsome price would command
a mansion in the depressed north-east of England and I started looking
in County Durham after work in the evenings. The estate agents were
depressing. I told them I wanted a four bedroom house with two
garages in a nice area. They sucked much air between teeth and shook
their heads. Three bedrooms, yes. Four bedrooms? Er, no, sorry, there
aren't any. My only chance would be a new house sometime in the
next six months, they said. That's ridiculous, I said, I will go and find
one. They laughed then, 'You'll be back for a three bedroom in a few
weeks,' they said. But they were right about four bedrooms. The only
four bedroom houses were currently under construction and the
demand was immense and extremely competitive. Apparently the
North-East had managed for some centuries with one, two and three
bedroom houses and it was only the influx of southern ponces who
demanded four bedrooms. I was to understand this fully only many
years later in interviewing a female employee concerning her regular
absence every Monday. The old joke in the pits was,

Outraged employer – 'Why do you only work four days a week?'

Unrepentant miner – 'Because I can't manage on three.'

I was determined the working culture of the pits was not coming into my factory.

'Tell me, is there some reason why you don't turn in for work every Monday?'

'It's because I get a bad neck on Mondays.'

'What? Only on Mondays?'

'Me brother's in the army, you see.'

Now I was no slouch at making vast leaps of understanding, usually with disastrous results, but the connection between her seasonal bad neck and her brother being in the army escaped me. I must be a bit slow today, I thought.

'I'm sorry, I don't understand. Why does your brother being in the army give you a bad neck every Monday?'

She looked at me with the sort of pity that a mother reserves for a stupid child.

'He's posted away to Aldershot, see.'

She paused, waiting for some understanding to dawn in the eyes of her inquisitor, and seeing none she continued in fine patronising style.

'Well, he comes home at weekends, see' – pause for it to sink in, 'An' he 'as to 'ave a bed. Me Ma' an' Da' 'ave one bedroom, the bairns 'ave the other an' he 'as to 'ave mine. I 'ave to sleep in the bath weekends' – pause,

'An' sleepin' in the bath gis me a bad neck!' she added in total exasperation.

See, three bedrooms was the limit in the North-East. The very concept of four bedrooms belonged with Einstein's General Theory of Relativity and the fourth dimension of quantum physics, vaguely heard of but best not contemplated too seriously lest your brain boil.

But I was getting desperate now. We were homeless by the end of January and after Annie's reaction to my last house purchase, I was determined to make no compromises.

Eventually, I fell to touring the many building companies who were building all over the North-East and at last I found a beautiful house deep in North Yorkshire in a small village development. It was almost forty miles from my work, and worse still, it was not scheduled for completion until May, the site office told me. I went to the

*14. My sister Dorothy with her two fine boys, George Jr. and David Michael.
Date uncertain but c. 1958, Wheatley Hills*

15. My sister Dorothy with her copy of The Thoughts of Chairman Mao, *c. 1990.
She once called me 'A running dog of a capitalist lackey', no doubt inspired by Chairman Mao*

16. Doncaster Grammar School 1956 aged 14. I am in the back row 6th from left

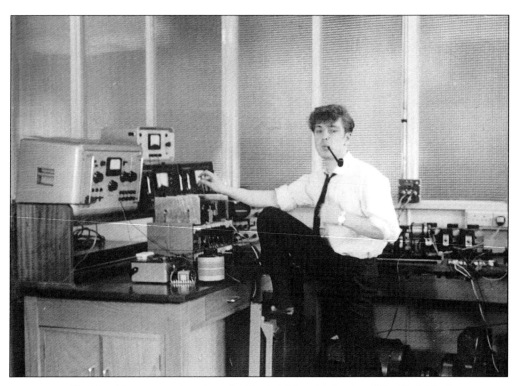

17. Me with my research project, the Tangled Mess. University of Bradford 1964

18. The happy children, Annie and me 1964

19. The happy children and parents 1964

20. Sisters – my mother Kathleen and her sister Rhoda. Holding hands at our wedding 1964

21. The legendary Al Decker, Spennymoor 1977

22. The Boardroom c. 1986

23. Annie and me with cup for Best Garden c. 1986. Annie did the garden too

24. Tuscany c. 1987

25. Annie, Mayor of Spennymoor for an hour, c. 1986

26. What the hell are you doing in the Labour Party? Spennymoor c. *1985*

27. The Prime Minister at Spennymoor 1987

28. Management Today, *September 1988. I am very tired.*

29. *Moscow 1995 with a member of the Russian State Symphony Orchestra moonlighting in a restaurant to feed his family*

builder's headquarters in Darlington and tried to negotiate an earlier completion. No chance, they said. At last, in desperation, I asked them to commit to complete by May in a contract. Equally no chance, it was a seller's market, and we were at an impasse. At that point the building manager got a phone call and left me in his office to take it. Around his office walls there were plans of all their scattered building developments, more than a dozen in all. The development plans had different coloured pins stuck into each property signifying completion and sale status. Idly glancing at the plans I suddenly saw a green pin. Hang on, didn't green mean finished and unsold? I checked the key in a fever of excitement now. Yup, there was a property completing within weeks and as yet unsold. It was one of fifteen houses arranged round a central green in what looked like a small village, decent plot, four bedrooms and two garages. Oh joy! I could hardly wait for the manager to get back. He verified my informed assumptions and I asked him where it was. Dalton Piercy, he said, only fourteen miles from the plant and with a town, Hartlepool, just five miles beyond. I took an immediate option on it and told him I would go and see it immediately and return within the day to formalise the purchase. And off I went. Dalton Piercy turned out to be a small farming village and the development was excellent and true to its rural location emphasised by the inclusion of a good village green in the centre of the development. It was perfect and I sped back to the builders and told them I would have it. This time I was confident that Annie would love it, but, not to take any chances, I arranged she would come down that weekend and give it her final seal of approval. She did. And that, children, is how you came to spend the next twenty-five formative years in County Durham in the bosom of Dalton Piercy: it was all down to coloured pins.

In the autumn of 1973, the miners and the government of Ted Heath were heading for their own impasse and soon there was an overtime ban by the miners, a state of emergency, and talk of a full blown miners' strike when industry would be limited to three days of production per week by law, a tragedy of disastrous economic proportions for the whole country, ultimately for the miners, and in prospect for Black and Decker under pressure as we were for production already. It was a good measure of the incisiveness of the Black and Decker management of the day that they refused to lie down and die for the miners as so many contemplated. They asked me if I could run the place on emergency generators. Too bloody right I could! This was home ground in a foreign land of processes I was still learning. The only problem was that we only had two emergency generators totalling 600 kW and the factory demand, even controlled and restricted, was nearly four times that. The Managing Director set about locating generating capacity but there was none to be had. All the UK stock had been snapped up by the essential services. Then he found an entrepreneur who proposed shipping generating sets in from the USA on cargo 747s straight to Heathrow. No frills, your own shipping beyond Heathrow, £75,000 each on delivery by certified banker's draft, take it or leave it. The price was ridiculous, the terms onerous but it was a sellers' market and we took it and I set about preparing the site for the miners' siege. We had three separate mains distribution boards which had to be linked in a ring main and we had to prepare sites and connections for the incoming generators. The lads set away with gusto. If you are ever caught with your back to the wall, get a good gang of Geordie lads with you; they love crisis and they are loyal and hard working and will fight to the last man. They were magnificent. While all this was going on I trained a core of my best in the rudiments of parallel generator operation, switching and synchronising, and what to do when things go wrong as indeed they must in such a stretched system. I organised 24 hour shift coverage for the power plant and included myself at the key times and finally prepared a set of instructions for production: like on no account start up the machine shop all at once, it would have to be phased in machine by machine.

Eventually we were all prepared and the new purchases turned up, two 750 kW diesel generating sets. I know they said there were no frills but they were basic in the extreme. The diesels were very good 12 cylinder Kohlers made in the good old US of A. The generators were tatty to say the least. Only one rotor bearing outboard, the inboard relying for support on the coupling and hence the diesel bearing, a design weakness just waiting to cause problems. There was only a rudimentary control board with just an isolating switch, a voltmeter and an ammeter, but no synchroscope. The whole lot was simply mounted on steel sleds but there was no cladding to weatherproof them. The lads set to work constructing wooden sheds to house them and I added a simple three-light system for synchronising them to the bus bars. We were finally ready and during the Christmas holiday, we had a dry run which was flawless in its execution. I was content we had done everything we could to prepare for the siege. Let the miners do their worst, my lads could hardly wait to go through their paces. They must have been the only small group in the whole of the UK who were actually looking forward to the fray.

And in January 1974, the miners did their worst and the country was plunged into industrial anarchy and semi-darkness. We maintained a five day week courtesy of our emergency generators and the Plant Engineering Tigers. It stretched on for months and I was getting tired. As well as my power plant rota duty, I maintained my departmental responsibilities in the day, sometimes just snatching a few hours sleep in the first aid room between daily office duty and a night shift. It didn't go without incident either. I had assigned an oiler and greaser to constantly go round the four generator sets checking for trouble free operation and keeping the fuel tanks topped up. One dark, frosty night he had just dipped one of the diesel engine's sump for oil when there was a mighty bang! and a 40 mm diameter gudgeon pin came straight through the cast steel sump housing and whistled by his ear barely a foot away. It's a great credit to him and the training we had given that despite his terrible fright he immediately threw the switch and shut down the generator otherwise the damage would have been terminal. As it was the remaining generators all followed and tripped out on overload, the factory plunged into sudden darkness.

'Why man, I'd just dipped the bloody thing when this big lump of steel shite came from nowhere an' bloody near took me 'ead off! Honest, it wasn't my fault.'

'You did fine, Jim. Next time wear this tin hat whenever tha's near one of the generators, and for God's sake catch the next piece of steel that jumps out on you. I don't want the next gudgeon pin damaged by hitting the ground like the last one.'

I got the manufacturers in with a flea in their ear and we took the sick diesel round to the press shop to get it under cover so they could work on it. The factory had to be re-jigged to run with 400 kW less supply and Genghis was not best pleased.

'This is most inconvenient. How long will it take them to repair it, David?'

'A week working twenty-four hours a day.'

'Don't be ridiculous! How can it possibly take seven days working twenty-four hours a day to repair a simple diesel engine?'

'Because it's a bloody big 12-cylinder in line, 400 kW diesel with major damage and it will be a bloody miracle if they manage it in that timescale.'

'I don't think you are putting enough pressure on them. I will speak to them.'

The last thing I needed was Genghis pissing off the repair crew who in any case had been reluctantly dragooned into going to the North-East in January to work twenty-four hours a day on a poxy diesel that would need a total strip down to get to the crankshaft. Right now I was satisfied they were moving at a frantic pace, not so much with our production in mind but rather to get out of a January County Durham as quickly as possible and back to the bosom of their family somewhere in the soft south.

It suddenly occurred to me that Genghis was thinking in terms of the only diesel engines he had ever come across in vans or cars. The sheer scale of a 12-cylinder, 400 kW diesel was totally alien to his finance education.

'Come and have a look at it,' I said, and he sullenly trooped after me through the factory to the press shop and a now largely dis-assembled monstrous diesel engine. Even dis-assembled, the body was massive: nearly three meters high and the crankshaft and pistons now lying on clean sheets around the monolith were clearly unliftable except with lifting gear.

'Bloody hell!' he said, and without another word turned on his heel and went back to the safety of his office and his columned numbers, suddenly grateful for the miracle of a week's deadline.

The design weakness in the newly purchased sets also came and bit our bums. Sure as day follows night, one of the couplings failed on full load having sheared the coupling bolts. This left the generator rotor to flail about on its one bearing until it tore through the insulation when there was a mighty bang and flash and the whole factory was out again.

The drawings said the coupling bolts should be high tensile steel. What remained of them didn't look like high tensile steel to me and I had them tested by metallurgists. Sure enough, they were mild steel and I raised hell with the suppliers. No sweat, they said, we'll ship you out a new set, and it will be there tomorrow. And it was.

I had one last run in with Genghis when a ceramic fuse fractured in the main medium voltage switchboard. The fuse was in the isolator arm of one of the generators and we couldn't switch in the generator until it was repaired. Bugger! To repair it we would have to get inside the switchboard with spanners and that meant a total shutdown to make the switchboard dead. I decided to repair it live. If I had ever caught my electricians doing the same thing, I would have fired them and I told them so. Nevertheless, I got them to bring a big, thick rubber mat to stand on, and then I carefully wrapped all my steel tools in a thick layer of insulating tape in case I dropped one and donned rubber gloves. I took off the switchboard cover at the offending switch exposing the arm and the 415 V bus bars and very gingerly started work removing the broken fuse. Right in the middle of all this the Tannoy requested David Fanthorpe to go to the General Manager's office. A summons to Genghis was not easily ignored but I was not about to leave this particular job unfinished. Eventually I had the new fuse installed and the panels replaced. The factory had been saved an expensive shutdown and I was unscathed, at least until I responded to the summons to Genghis' office. With one last censure to the small team who had helped me that this was an exercise never to be repeated at peril of their jobs, I went off to my meeting with Genghis at least half an hour after the last call. When I got there, I found the Company Director of Personnel there as well and Genghis was quietly furious.

'Why didn't you come when I asked?'

I apologised and told him a sanitised version of the preceding events.

'Why didn't you get your engineers to do it?' he persisted.

'Because they are not bloody well qualified to do it. It was dangerous and I'm the only professional electrical engineer in this whole bloody company if you hadn't noticed!' I answered with the venom of the weary.

In my tired state I was close to losing my temper with him and the Director of Personnel, ever one to pour oil on troubled waters, intervened nervously on my behalf.

'Now come on, that had to be David's decision. Let's get on.'

But that only incensed Genghis the more and a blazing row developed, in which I gave as much as I took. Eventually it fizzled out and we got on with the discussions I had been originally summoned to.

By and large though, the whole campaign went remarkably well
and my little band of newly qualified power station engineers had
carried the day when the miners eventually went back to work. And
it hadn't gone unnoticed by my colleagues and even by Genghis.
There was a new respect for the commitment of and the contribution
from Plant Engineering. 'It's an ill wind that blows no good' was
never truer and ambition burned.

CHAPTER 5

Production man at large

Production men – it's mainly true –
Have lacked respect to which they're due
As if to spend their time with spanners
Left slightly questionable manners

Bertie Ramsbottom: 'The Dirty Handed Tons of Soil'
from *The Bottom Line*

THE NEXT FEW YEARS went quickly. I loved every minute of it: the varied work, the management team interplay and the whole ethos of the Company. In my memory the years were only punctuated by periodic promotions as I was exposed to ever widening functions in the business and by major political events. In 1976 the Wilson Labour Government introduced a new Employment Act which, among other things, involved the right of Unions to be recognised in companies by law. The situation in Black and Decker remained an affront to the Unions and the new Act gave a fresh impetus to their efforts to represent our employees. The ethos in the Company was largely governed by the way that management related to all employees. They were to be treated as individuals and scrupulously fairly at all times. Every quarter, the whole factory was stopped and the General Manager addressed all the employees throughout the twenty-four hour shifts. He would tell them the good news and the bad news and talk about the challenges of the coming quarter. Once per year, this briefing would include news of the wage review and annual pay rise with the rationale behind the number. Throughout the year any employee had the right to take a grievance or comment all the way up the management chain if he so wished, culminating in a meeting with the Chairman if that's what it took. Woe betide the Manager who was found to be treating an employee without the proper respect for his views or denying him his right of prompt access to senior management if it was required. It was a company ethos I had never come across before and it was an enlightenment of massive proportion. I loved the simplicity of it, the lack of animosity in grievances and political infighting between

Management and Unions. The employees valued it too. Despite the Unions organising a campaign, reinvigorated by the 1976 Employment Act, in the press and at our gates, the employees for the most part feared any outcome that would involve recognition of the Unions. So the Company organised a secret ballot of all employees supervised by the Electoral Reform Society, in which we were all asked whether we wanted to be represented by the Unions. The result was a resounding 'No' with 82 per cent voting against Union recognition, and the Unions went away again with a bloody nose, bruised but still not defeated and they grumbled on remorselessly.

Sometimes unique experiences were put my way at this time. One was a trip to India where Black and Decker had a joint venture with an Indian company making and selling power tools. It had been a troublesome joint venture with continuing poor results and a crunch was approaching. I was asked to go and re-evaluate the joint venture company with a view to dissolving the partnership.

I landed at Bombay on a Saturday night and found my hotel. *The Times of India* was filled with a story about 'police blindings' which I found very confusing at first. Apparently it was a long running story involving some brutal policing and an alleged government cover-up. The more I read, the more I understood. Allegedly some organised crime thugs had been kidnapped by the police (or was that arrested?) and because they couldn't prove the allegations against the big time criminals, the police, in their frustration, had spirited the criminals away into the country and taken their eyes out. Subsequent official enquiries had vindicated the police and hence the political furore. Bloody hell! A clip round the ear in a police station is one thing, but taking your eyes out? A little extravagant, I think. I made a mental note to steer well clear of the fearsome Bombay police. Welcome to a totally different world. During Sunday my host took me on a tour of Bombay which only reinforced the brutally different world I was now in. Beggars, horribly maimed in the most disfiguring way they could invent, were everywhere, and the most heartrending thing of all, children, mostly girls, as young as four abandoned to fend for themselves on the streets of Bombay. I tried to ignore the deprivation as Englishmen abroad tend to do out of politeness to their hosts but at the Gateway to India, thronged with tourists and residents, I felt a tug on my elbow. Looking down I saw a beautiful girl, no more than four, with the biggest, roundest brown eyes I had ever seen. She was begging and, deeply moved, I went for my wallet. My host saw what was happening and callously ordered her away with a vicious kick.

'No Sir! If you do that we will never solve our homeless problem,' he said, 'and you will be besieged with beggars.'

To my shame, I let this pass in deference to my host. Casual violence and indifference seemed to be an acceptable part of this world.

The joint venture was down in Kulapur, three hundred miles south of Bombay. How to get there had been problematical from the beginning. I consulted the Marketing Manager who had paid periodic visits to the partnership.

'Well, there is an air service from Bombay, a train service, or you can get someone to drive you down. I've done them all. They all have their drawbacks. I once flew down in the monsoon season, but the Captain couldn't find the airstrip, it had grown over you see, and he had to return to Bombay. On the other hand, the trains are a nightmare. They systematically double book and chances are your seat will be taken when you get to the train. You can't drive in India, it's too dangerous for a European. You need special skills, you see.'

Very bloody useful that, I wonder what the special skills are, I thought. I took my courage in both hands and flew down. Sure enough, the 'airport' was a dirt strip with a tin shed for Arrivals and Departures and an Indian native driver there to meet me. With much bowing and scraping he ran to the car with my bags, his bare feet slapping on the concrete. I then discovered the special skills required to drive in India in the 1980s. Most roads, even main roads, were quite narrow. To make matters worse, they were so badly maintained that there was only one car width negotiable for both directions of traffic. The technique was to drive headlong down the only navigable bit, blasting the horn and flashing headlights at the oncoming traffic who, not unreasonably, wanted to use the same bit of road as you. A few seconds before impact, one or other of the drivers would 'chicken out' and swerve violently into the deep potholes to avoid oblivion. The 'special skill' was an iron nerve and an almost total suppression of the will to live. By the time we got to my hotel, the Pearl of Kulapur, I was beyond terror and I tried to open the car door with shaking hand. The driver was outraged.

'No, no, Sahib! I must open door. You wait. I wery quick.'

I tried to carry my briefcase into the hotel lobby while the driver brought my bags. He was doubly outraged and even hurt that I wouldn't let him carry the briefcase.

'Oh dear oh dear oh dear, Sahib! I must carry cases, Sahib go and rest!'

I gave in and he padded after me with armfuls of bags and a self satisfied smile. He would have his Sahib whipped into shape in no time.

The first day in the factory was hard work. It was very hot and I was still suffering jetlag. The factory itself was rudimentary. Most operations were carried out by hand. Where we took machinery for granted, for them any machine was a major investment and labour so cheap that it made good financial sense to do things manually. The factory didn't seem very busy though, just a few women squatting on the floor fettling castings and other menial tasks. I commented on this and the owner shamefacedly told me the factory was on strike. Apparently whenever a European manager visited an Indian joint venture, the employees always went on strike for higher pay. When the European asked what they were paid and it turned out to be less than 10 cents per hour, they often said, 'Oh, give them what they are asking for,' the relevance of a 10 per cent pay rise on 10 cents per hour lost on them. So it was always worth a try when the Sahib came to town.

'You can tell them from me that I will have absolutely nothing to do with the internal affairs of this company. They are wasting their time,' I said and got on with my work interviewing all the functional managers one by one.

By six in the evening, I was very tired and ready to call it a day. But the owners kept putting new people in front of me and eventually I had to tell them that I was very tired and jetlagged, not to mention hot, sweaty and smelling, and I really would like to go to my hotel. Nothing happened. They kept wheeling in new people to interview oblivious to my earlier request. Eventually, I got quite sharp with them and told them in no uncertain terms to take me to my hotel. The awful truth then unfolded. With immense shame, they told me that I couldn't leave the plant. The strikers were mobbing the factory gates, and if they tried to drive me through, the strikers would lie down in the road to prevent it. Treble bugger! The thought of spending the night in this hell hole was too much to bear.

'What!? Well, what's to be done? I'm not staying here all night; I'd rather poke my eyes with red hot needles!' I said, and then remembered the Bombay police and their careless expertise with eyes. My unthinking alternative could surely be arranged if I wasn't careful.

'Oh no, Sahib. We have applied to the High Court to have the strike declared illegal. The case is being heard now. When the judge rules, the police will clear away the strikers, arrest the ringleaders, take them out to the country and break their legs. It will be fine in just a short time.'

Now as anxious as I was to vacate the squalid factory for my squalid hotel, I couldn't countenance such sanctions, and I told them so in no uncertain terms, and in due course, I was driven to my hotel, strikers' legs still intact, or so I hoped. The terror of a night drive with my nerveless driver wiped out all the day's events at least for the duration of the drive and I surrendered to the tender mercies of the Pearl of Kulapur, its curries and its mosquitoes.

After ten days I was finished. I knew all I hoped to know about the Indian power tool market, the joint venture partners and their manufacturing, and not a little bit more than I cared to know about India. On my last night down in Kulapur, my hosts threw a party for me at their family farm, a sugar cane plantation. They had a huge bonfire of spent sugar cane and a barbeque. During my stay in India, I had heeded all the good advice about not taking ice with drinks, not eating salad or indeed any uncooked food, and I had been fine. This last night I threw caution to the winds, helped, no doubt, by copious amounts of homemade rum, a by-product of sugar cane farming. I ate corn on the cob roasted in the sugar cane bonfire (I can recommend this as one of those experiences only to be had in foreign lands), salad with my curry and vast amounts of home-made rum. At the end of the evening, I felt full of bonhomie, replete and ready to hug the next person who crossed my double vision.

My hosts dropped me at the Pearl of Kulapur and I slept the sleep of the good while getting the host of mosquitoes drunk on their nightly feast of my blood. I woke next morning with the severest of hangovers, and worse, a very bad case of the Delhi bellies, facing a 300-mile trip up to Bombay by car and the prospect of no Public Conveniences worth the name for the whole 300 miles. It wouldn't take the drive of terror up the Indian A1 cart track to force the crap out of me this time.

'Quick, quick! Where's the toilet?'

'From here to the sea, Sahib.'

I made some changes to my itinerary. I was supposed to be going to Agra and the Taj Mahal, and then meeting with the Government Minister responsible for Marahashtra State, before flying out of Bombay three days later. I cancelled the trip to Agra and Delhi, made my heartfelt apologies to the minister and headed up the A1 for Bombay and an early flight home. Somehow I endured the drive up to Bombay and eventually settled into my Bombay hotel, a very swish place with the new fangled 'air conditioning'. Next day I was feeling a little better and even ate dinner. After dinner I took a stroll along the seafront promenade outside. As I walked, an Indian came pattering after me and eventually caught up.

'You want marijuana, Sahib?'

'No, thank you very much,' and I quickened my pace.

'You want heroin then, Sahib?' he said, pattering after me.

'NO! I do not.'

He was puzzled now, so he tried a different tack.

'You want woman then, Sahib? I get you fine woman.'

'NO I DO NOT! Now go away please!'

'Ah!' he said, beaming, having eliminated all other possibilities as to where my appetites lay, 'You want man.'

I stopped, looked him squarely in the eyes and told him as viciously as I could that I wanted none of these things and if he didn't go away, I would call the fearsome Bombay Police. He looked deeply hurt and even disappointed in himself that he had failed to identify the one appetite in me that he could satisfy for our mutual gain. I left him scratching his head in bewilderment at his failure but relieved he wouldn't be losing his eyes or his legs so long as he left me alone, and finished my stroll.

My flight back to London was at some ungodly hour in the early morning, so I checked out of the hotel about midnight.

'You are using a taxi, Sir?'

'Yes.'

'Then be sure to tell your driver that you know the way to the airport and that you want to go straight there. No detours, tell him. And the fare should be no more than 100 rupees.'

I thanked the receptionist for his advice and walked out to the magnificent, turbaned concierge waiting with my bags outside. Taxis were lined up at a discreet distance waiting for business. The magnificent concierge blew his whistle imperiously as a summons, whereupon a taxi from the back of the hopeful queue broke ranks and screeched to a halt in front of us before the first taxi in the queue could even engage first gear. The driver began loading my bags into the boot of his battered Morris Ambassador, but the outraged driver whose business I should properly have been arrived behind the renegade driver. A furious argument developed and my bags oscillated from one taxi to the other as each driver claimed me as their rightful business. The concierge remonstrated with them loudly and grandly, whereupon a full scale fist fight broke out between the two drivers. At this point, half my bags were in one taxi, and half in the other. The concierge wasn't going to sully his magnificent uniform or his dignity by intervening; instead, he blew his whistle in a series of short blasts and I soon realised the purpose. Around the corner came one of Bombay's finest, a member of the fearsome Bombay constabulary. He set about the two brawlers with his long bamboo baton, beating them about the head and shoulders until the rain of blows from the baton exceeded the blows aimed at each other, and they stopped fighting. Bombay's finest quickly arbitrated the dispute and my bags were consolidated into the rightful taxi and with a salute from the constable and the concierge we were off. My driver was a sorry sight. Even more dishevelled than a normal Bombay taxi driver, he had blood still running from the cuts on his head and a real shiner developing. Feeling sorry for him, I told him very politely that I knew where the airport was and I was in a hurry, so no detours please.

'Oh yes, yes, Sahib. I'm wery fine driver. I get you there wery quick! And we careered on through largely deserted Bombay streets. I was beginning to regret telling him I was in a hurry. He screamed round bends and overtook whatever traffic he came across regardless of oncoming vehicles but eventually got stuck behind a lorry. The road widened and he began overtaking the lorry. His old Morris Ambassador was just about clapped out, and he was barely making any progress past the lorry at all so lorry and taxi careered through the night side by side. At least there's no oncoming traffic, I thought, but then, in the distance I could see the highway we were on changing to a dual carriageway, with room for only one vehicle in each direction. There was no way he would get by the lorry before the traffic island intervened but he was totally unconcerned, as opposed to me with my Delhi belly suddenly reactivated. Now I definitely regretted telling him I was in a hurry. The traffic island duly separated the lorry from my taxi as we sped down the wrong side of the dual carriageway.

Then in the far distance, headlights appeared. 'It's OK!' I wanted to shout, 'I don't mind missing my flight so long as it's not because I'm in the Bombay General Hospital!' but I was struck dumb. The headlights closed on us rapidly, though it seemed like forever. Then horns and flashing headlights were drawn and the usual Indian duel of the road ensued until at the very last second, my driver swerved off the road and onto the pavement without benefit of brakes, and we careered on to the airport, my driver smugly pleased with himself and me in a cold sweat.

'Three hundred rupees, Sahib,' said my driver.

'The hotel said it should be one hundred rupees!' I replied.

Caught out in his attempted fraud and with the Bombay constabulary hovering just up the concourse, he immediately became an abject wretch, wailing and bowing in total submission and obeisance.

'Oh I am so, so sorry, Sahib. I didn't mean to cheat you. I am so wery, wery sorry, Sahib. Please, please forgive,' and on and on he went. I suddenly felt very ashamed for my meanness. After all, he had got me here in record time, suffered cuts and bruises for the privilege, the blood from which was still running down his face and in all other respects had been of exemplary service.

'It's OK. Please get up. You can have three hundred rupees,' I said.

His face was immediately wreathed in a bloody grin. He had won again. The Sahibs were so easy! And so I left India. Despite all, I loved the country and its people but I had truly experienced another world.

In 1979, the Company demonstrated its commitment to me and my future with them even more roundly. They said they would like me to do a General Management course in one of the UK Business Schools. I was allowed to pick which school and eventually I went to do an eight week residential course in General Management. I couldn't believe my luck, or the generosity of Black and Decker in providing training of such expense. The General Management course was amazing. Finance, Accounting, Business Strategy, Human Resource Management and much else all packed into eight intensive residential weeks in which we were often worked until late at night. I loved it and just soaked it all up. Any lingering regrets about not doing a Masters in Business Administration at Bradford were now dispelled. I was now armed with management tools which complemented my technical training in an engineering based company and I had no doubts as to Black and Decker's commitment to my future career with them.

Genghis had long since ascended to greater things, first to the UK Managing Director role then into Europe as European President. In his absence we had a succession of 'visiting' General Managers, temporarily and reluctantly seconded from jobs at head office to fill the gap left by Genghis. Their commitment to the plant was questionable and in any case they were only there three days a week so it was a very unsatisfactory arrangement for everybody. The Company obviously wanted to make a permanent replacement, but none of us incumbents had the necessary experience, at least until now. Eventually, the company king maker descended on the plant from head office. He wanted to take Annie and me out to dinner one night, and a good colleague and his wife the next night. Clearly, though it went unsaid, choices were being made. An engineer had never become a General Manager in Black and Decker before, commercial and accounting types always being preferred, so I was still an outside bet. As far as I recall, the dinner went reasonably well and without incident, but a week later, my colleague, a commercial type, was appointed General Manager and I was bitterly disappointed. I liked my colleague immensely and I had always got on very well with him. I had to be pleased for him for that alone, but still, I wondered if an engineer would ever make the grade. I got a partial answer. In his re-shuffle the new General Manager appointed me General Manufacturing Manager and I got Production thrown into my pot. At least I was now a production man and clearly the heir apparent.

And further more, for what it's worth,
By very nature of his birth,
An engineer was thought to be
From social classes two or three,
So not, like some among his peers,
At Eton in his former years;
Hence lacking in the social graces
Required for elevated places

Too long, we chose to favour trade
To what is actually made;
As if to handle a machine
Were, in some curious way, obscene;
While finance, stocks and shares, or shipping
Were, oh! So marvellously ripping!

Bertie Ramsbottom: 'The Dirty Handed Tons of Soil'
from *The Bottom Line*

Then serious illness intervened. I was going to a meeting in
Washington but the early Teesside flight didn't turn up and I missed
my Heathrow connection to Washington. By the time I got to
Heathrow, all the Washington flights had left and I had to re-route
via New York where I would have to overnight before catching an
early flight from there to Washington. Treble bugger! I had to change
airlines and tickets, I would miss the start of the meeting and I would
have to clear immigration in JFK which is less than a pleasant
experience.

I arrived in New York at about 11.00 p.m. and went straight to bed
having eaten well on the trans-Atlantic flight. In the early hours I was
awakened by violent belly-ache, vomiting and diarrhoea. I hardly slept
the rest of the night but I presumed it would all burn itself out given a
little time as hundreds of belly-aches had done before. I dragged myself
back to the airport and onto my Washington flight and onward to my
meeting which was scheduled to last three days. Instead of getting
better, it got worse. On the second day, I made my excuses and headed
for home. It was a nightmare trip. I daren't tell the airline I was ill,
otherwise they might not carry me. I sought a seat strategically located
next to the toilets in Business Class and endured the seven-hour flight
back to the UK, lapsing into fitful sleep whenever I could. Eventually, I
arrived home, so weak I could barely walk, let alone tote my bag, and a
concerned Annie put me to bed. She called our GP but he wouldn't
come out. After some of Annie's choice and selective Irish invective, he
agreed to see me down at his surgery and Annie drove me down. The
doctor made the usual abdominal examinations and asked me where I
had been. I told him the USA, and he immediately called a halt to any
further investigation. 'You've been eating something too rich for you!'
he said, and prescribed Immodium. 'You'll be fine in a day or two.'

But I wasn't. The bug in my belly just loved the Immodium and
prospered on the unusual feast arriving every four hours, and I got

worse. Eventually even the GP became concerned and the hospital diagnosed salmonella food poisoning. Not that this was much help. They said there were no drugs that would reach it and that I would have to starve it out. Three weeks later and twenty pounds lighter, I finally beat the damned thing and started to eat cautiously. By then, the origins of the poison were known. It was the airline food. They had managed to poison seven humdred people that day with a contaminated aspic glaze that went onto almost every meal served. My next door neighbour who was an Indian orthopaedic surgeon enquired as to what had happened and I told him the airline had given me salmonella.

'Some damn native has given you this!' said Sidhu my neighbour, 'their catering kitchens are bloody full of them down at Heathrow.' He should know, I thought.

It was lucky that I was very fit at the time, running six miles per day and playing squash regularly, otherwise I might not have recovered so completely, maybe not at all. It was as ill as I had ever been and it made me treasure every day afresh.

We had a new Chairman and Managing Director by now, another bloody accountant. Worse still, he had been European Treasurer before this appointment. Just what we bloody need! An esoteric finance guy; they don't come more esoteric, even in accountancy, than treasurers. But I was wrong. Roger turned out to be one of the most remarkable General Managers and Chairmen I ever met. He came up to the Spennymoor manufacturing plant as part of his induction. He confessed with brutal honesty that he knew nothing of manufacturing, but he would make it his first priority to learn, and he did. He came up every week for the next six months, spending three days per week on his manufacturing training, a massive commitment in his bursting diary. He had us organise a programme of visits to every department in the plant, where he would immerse himself in the functional speciality led by the functional manager. He had a massive capacity for relevant detail and a good intellect to take on his new understandings. At the end of his six months he could have made a good fist of running any of the individual specialities and he had earned massive respect from the battle hardened and cynical manufacturing crew. Over the years, he proved to have massive talents in Marketing, New Product and Business Strategy all tempered by realism, a combination that I had never encountered before. He also had a very good eye for aesthetics and he applied it not just to new products but to the appearance of the manufacturing plant as well. We used to think that this was an unnecessary extravagance, a frippery in a production plant. But we were wrong again. All the improvements in the plant appearance gradually engendered a feeling of new pride in the place throughout all the employees. As Mastercard would say:

Planting hedging and flower beds	£10,000
Tinted glass in the new conference rooms	£15,000
Painting aisles and working areas different colours	£10,000
Pride in your workplace	Priceless

Armed by his new knowledge and growing in confidence he took comprehensive command of the company and began to make big changes. He re-invigorated the new product programme, increased the staffing in Design Engineering by relocating existing resources so they were up and running immediately. He insisted on precise definitions of all the administration processes and they were much improved as a result. He insisted that all new management recruitment should be guided by looking for the best, a good rule of thumb being 'Look for someone who has at least the potential to be better than you.' We were in very good hands and I learned more about general management from him than I had taken from Business School and all that had gone before.

In 1984 my General Manager, Ken, moved on to his preference in running a Marketing Company abroad, and became Managing Director of Black and Decker France, a move that would have tragic consequences. The Chairman appointed me as the first engineer to be General Manager Spennymoor with full profit responsibility and New Product Development within my remit. I had my own command at last. It was a big stretch, but I was determined I was going to change the Black and Decker manufacturing and product development world for the good. Then came chilling and tragic news which killed all enthusiasm for some time.

In April 1986, Ken Marston was shot and killed on his own doorstep by an assassin wearing a black ski mask at his house in Lyon. It was assumed at first that it was the work of Arab terrorists in a reprisal for the American bombing of Libya, and Special Branch visited us to warn of possible further attacks. I was told to vary my route into the office from home and to check for car bombs whenever my car had been left unattended. The whole of the factory were devastated by the news. Ken had been a very popular General Manager, a truly decent family man and a very good personal friend. Clearly, our distress was as nothing to that of his wife and family who had been in the house at the time of the shooting. They were inconsolable and I suspect, remain so to this day.

We were forbidden by corporate ban to attend his funeral in Lyon for security reasons, and I tried to hold the company line with my management team, all of them good friends of the family. I faced open revolt and eventually we defied the corporate ban and went to Lyon, helped by the UK Managing Director who bravely countermanded the corporate edict to allow us to go. I have never been to a sadder, more heart-rending funeral and I cried uncontrollably at the service.

Months later Special Branch returned to tell us that they now knew for certain that Arab terrorists were not involved and they were now following a criminal enquiry. How they could be so certain remains known only to them and their secret world. Despite a multi-million dollar reward put up by the corporation, no-one was ever arrested for the murder, and the motive remains a mystery to this day, a source of constant distress to Ken's family and especially his widow. Goodbye old friend, and damn the blackhearted bastard who committed such a foul thing.

CHAPTER 6

The rising sun

Research and Development

Internally the group comprises
Those in line for Nobel Prizes;
And a lesser group who lurk
Around to make the damn thing work.
The former sit, and think, and stammer;
The latter stand with wrench and hammer

Both go wobbly at the knees
At mention of the Japanese

Bertie Ramsbottom: *The Bottom Line*

IN THE 1980S, THE JAPANESE were in industrial ascendancy and putting the fear of God into all of Western industry. They had already decimated the Western machine tool industry and were three quarters of the way to decimating Detroit and the Western automobile industry. They were doing it with quality that was then unknown to Western manufacturers, with product innovation, with price and with a growing marketing skill. Clearly they had something we had not in their factories and businesses. Most commentators in the west said it was robots. Trade magazines, Government research and newspapers were full of tables showing the number of robots per head of working population in Japan, the USA and in Britain. The tables invariably showed that we British had the fewest, the Japanese the most and then correlated this with our diminishing world trade share. There are lies, damned lies and statistics (Benjamin Disraeli, later, Mark Twain) and this particular correlation always seemed a bit unlikely to me. It was never that easy, of that I was sure.

Black and Decker Corporate in the USA were getting particularly concerned at the Japanese menace. They had enjoyed decades of market supremacy with the B&D brand but it was under growing threat from Makita and Hitachi who had made inroads in the US market, particularly in professional power tools. It hadn't happened in Europe yet, but I was under no illusion that what happened in America today would happen in Britain tomorrow, it was always so.

So it was that in September 1983, corporate headquarters in America commanded a study tour of Japanese industry, put together by a prominent Management Consultancy, and I was dispatched to join it with two European colleagues, one from France and one from Germany. It was an intensive seventeen-day tour of the very best of Japanese manufacturers, intellectuals and trade shows, and it was devastating. What we found was a totally alien business culture, a fanatical dedication to success in ALL the population and methodologies that were so innovative that they defied immediate understanding. Total Quality, Just In Time, (JIT as opposed to JTFL in our factories. JTL stands for Just Too Late, I'll leave you to fill in the rest), Kan Ban and a hundred others all applied with massive universal industry by the Japanese population in general. I returned from the trip jetlagged and bilious with three burning questions, utterly convinced that unless we answered them rigorously, and acted on them just as rigorously, we would not survive the Japanese threat

1. How do we address the issue of customer orientating our company to the same degree as Japanese companies?
2. How do we address the issue of fanatical commitment to quality in its comprehensive Japanese sense, to enable us to contain the Japanese on this single front alone?
3. How, within our Western cultural values, do we motivate our employees to make similar contributions to the business success as Japanese employees do for theirs?'

I'm sorry to bore you with dry business liturgy, but that visit to Japan had such a profound effect on the rest of my business life and attitudes to work that in part, it is what made me what I am.

Some years later I got another reminder of Japanese ruthlessness in business. We were trying to negotiate a global contract for the supply of a key electronic component with a household name Japanese company. The negotiations had been long, tedious and difficult and culminated in a final meeting between us and them to resolve the issue. The Japanese turned up mob handed as they usually did and in anticipation; we had a good team out too. We sat at a big round table, Japanese team on one side and our team on the other. After a long day's negotiation we were finally getting somewhere when a junior member of the Japanese team interjected with a negative attitude. Bugger! We were back to square one. In the silence that followed, the Japanese MD got up and slowly and deliberately walked round the table to his naysayer. Then without a word, he slapped the poor man round the back of his head with such a crack! it startled everybody. He walked just as slowly back to his chair and resumed the negotiation where we had left off as if nothing had happened. We were back on track, and the hapless junior spent the rest of the meeting with his head deeply bowed in shame and never uttered another word. I later told my team that I was seriously considering the Japanese example when someone disagreed with me in public.

I took these Damascene experiences with me when, a year later, I got my own command as General Manager, Manufacturing UK, and answering the three questions of my report became the template for my watch in the hot seat. I had a truly great team on my manufacturing board. Eddie, a Scouser tempered in the fires of Liverpool industry, the Rock and Roll clubs of Hamburg and Anfield, was my Director of Personnel and he embraced the challenge of getting the extra million miles from all our employees with a wit and humour only matched by his innovative approach to human resource management. At the end of every long hard day, Eddie would come through to my office and we would chew the fat on how things were going, the latest factory scandals – or at least those he thought the General Manager should know about – and new ideas for advancing employee relations, and I would wend my weary way home about eight o'clock to the patient Annie and the bosom of my family.

Then there was Brian in Engineering, an older wiser man in many respects but a brilliantly innovative design engineer blessed with a talent for getting the best from that peculiar animal The Designer. He counterbalanced the occasional unworldliness of designer types with practicality and realism and the new products were better and prompter as a result. The two of them have remained lifelong friends long after we all hung up our boots.

All my functional Directors were excellent, committed business-men. They made the difference in the following years and in the revolution that was unleashed by the Japanese threat. They were a great tribute to past recruitment policies and I was lucky to have them.

In the next five years, we transformed the factory and design centre. We gave the revolution an easy name and said we were building 'The Factory of the Future', their factory of the future, so it became owned by everybody. We tore down the grading structure and replaced it with simple, rationalised, broadly defined grades that linked management grades with shop floor grades, no more them and us; we brought in Quality Circles but in our own guise as Total Customer Service groups; we automated the manufacturing processes and design engineering with computer aided design; we designed and introduced our own computer stock control system and trained and trained and trained. Some of the 'training' was a little unorthodox. I got very impatient with the traditional scruffiness of the workforce. The factory always looked untidy and even dirty. After weeks of entreaties, threats and even near violence, I lost my temper with it. I took a camera and made fifty photographs of the general disarray and had the apprentices mount them on a big board, and then I had it located in our boardroom with a cover on it. At our next manufacturing operating committee, I unveiled it and forced the managers to witness their own areas faithfully reproduced in photographs in all their degrading detail. I berated the poor managers without mercy. 'Is this what your Factory of the Future is supposed to look like?' I asked them. Heads fell with shame. I never had problems with the plant housekeeping after that.

Every single employee was required to become computer literate. Apprentices were henceforth to be dual skilled in electrical and mechanical engineering to degree level. If they were good, they got the best sandwich courses going. The maintenance craftsmen were required to become at least dual skilled and technicians rather than craftsmen.

To train the apprentices in leadership we took them on Outward Bound long weekends in the Lake District led by managers and they were a great success. We would take them out on long treks and assigned individual apprentices to lead the group in various sections of the trek. The weekends were instructive and immensely enjoyable and helped form a bond between the managers and their putative talent base, the apprentices. It exposed managers as well as the trainees to new aspects of relationship and leadership but it didn't always go according to plan.

One March the first trip was typical. It was a beautiful spring day down in the valleys, clear and sunny, but there was still a snow line up in the mountains. We arrived on Friday afternoon and after stowing our gear in the mountain hut we were using for the expedition, we retired, as you do, to the nearest pub. Several pints later at closing time we returned to our hut to find it crowded with newcomers, all attracted out by the wonderful spring weather after a long dark northern winter. Lucky we had arrived so early, I thought, at least we had bunk beds to pitch our sleeping bags on. Most of the newcomers weren't so lucky and the floor was strewn with sleeping bags, their incumbents sound asleep in readiness for the day's adventures to come. We tiptoed through the maze of sleeping bodies and took to our bunks. I stripped off naked to climb into my sleeping bag to keep my outdoor clothes as fresh as possible, though others treated smelling like a pole-cat as a badge of honour on these weekends. The hut was pretty basic. At one end was an open space with worktops and a big pot bellied stove which had been well fired up by the newcomers so that it was subtropical inside the hut. At the other end were ranks of three-story bunk beds where we early birds were to sleep.

I settled down to sleep sweating profusely in my sleeping bag but helped to sleep no end by the five pints of Guinness consumed down at the pub. They were my undoing. At about 3.00 a.m. I woke desperately needing the lavatory, the five pints of Guinness requiring immediate egress. Fine, except there wasn't one. You had to go outside and pee in the stream. I extracted myself from my sleeping bag and trod gingerly between the sleeping bodies without waking anyone and went out. It was a crystal clear, star lit night and frost glistened in the moonlight. Stark naked, this was intimidating to say the least, but needs must, and the effects of the Guinness helped. I completed my business and pranced urgently back to the hut. The door I had come out from had closed behind me and it was only then I discovered it had a Yale lock which had latched on closing. Bugger! I was locked out and rapidly turning blue with the cold. I searched round the hut for an open window, but found none. The hut and its sub-tropical climate were virtually hermetically sealed against the weather. I contemplated how to get back in. There was nothing for it, I would have to knock on the door until somebody awoke and opened the door from the inside. This decision did not come easily. Knocking on the door would almost certainly wake the entire population, who would not be best pleased. But that was as nothing compared to the ridicule I would attract making my ignominious entry, stark naked, blue, and with my manhoods shrivelled into almost non existence. I spent another few minutes desperately trying to think of another solution. If I had my credit card, I would be able to slip the Yale lock, but there weren't any to be found in the wilds of Langdale and there certainly wasn't any secreted about my naked person. Eventually I gave up and brought my fist back to give the door a good desperate rap. In mid swing, the door miraculously opened and there stood one of my junior managers in similar attire to myself and bent on the same errand.

'Jesus Christ almighty!' he said. 'You frightened the crap out of me.'

Not being in the mood to dally in the frosty moonlight, I scurried past him telling him as I went not to let the door close behind him. Miraculously, none of the other campers had stirred and I was soon back inside my sleeping bag to let the now welcome warmth of the sub-tropical interior soak into my frozen extremities.

The expedition next day was the ascent of Scafell Pike and we made a good start down the valley and up into the fells below Scafell in glorious sunshine led by the first nominee apprentice. It was to be a long walk as the group leaders made a couple of navigational mistakes so it was some hours later when we started the final ascent up Scafell Pike, the highest mountain in England. The party was getting tired, especially the apprentices, and a weary silence descended on the group as we toiled Indian file up the mountainside through the snowline. Gone was the cheeky banter and jokes, heads were now down and the pace plodding. Then, about 500 feet from the summit, we passed an extraordinary sight. A man in full mountain gear, ice pick and crampons, was disrobing by the side of the steep track. He was changing into full black tie evening dress. Such was the weariness of my party that even this bizarre sight failed to raise a comment and we passed the sartorial gent without as much as a backward glance. Finally, we rounded the last rock to reveal the summit and trig point. If the man changing into evening dress was bizarre, the sight that greeted us at the summit was surreal. A butler in full regalia had set out his silver tray on a crisp white tablecloth on the trig point marker, and from his tray he was serving champagne to an assembly of ladies and gentlemen all in formal evening dress, the ladies in long evening gowns. A buzz of happy chat and laughter came from the group as they exchanged party small talk. Bloody hell!

Altitude sickness can do strange things, but we weren't nearly high enough for that. There had to be a rational or indeed irrational explanation. I talked to the jolly band. They were medical students from one of the universities, and this was their Mad March Hare party. Of course! It was 1 March. What else would you do for a 1 March party?

My apprentices took a great lift from this and their successful conquest of Scafell and soon the banter had returned as we wove our way back down the mountain to the joys of our mountain hut and a hot meal cooked on the pot bellied stove. Their only complaint now was that the butler had refused to serve them champagne.

Back at the factory the revolution progressed and sometimes with comical overtones. We tested all employees for aptitudes and skills and gave them a place in the rationalised grading system according to their results. One of the tests was a simple intelligence test. You know the sort of thing:

'If a train leaves Station A at 10 miles per hour, and another train leaves station B, ten miles away, in the opposite direction and travels at 10 miles per hour, how long will it take for the trains to meet?'

There was outrage in the Assembly Shop girls:

'How do I bloody kna' when they'll bloody meet. Ah've nevva bin to Station A! All ah kna' is they're bloody slow trains, ah could wark it as fast. Bloody silly question!'

This was reported to me by my Secretary Ruth who was a mine of information on the scuttlebutt from the Ladies loo. It was clear that some of our ideas needed a bit more work before launching them on an astonished North-East population.

But the revolution continued. We redesigned the product so that we could automate its assembly and we bought the best Swiss and German machine tools to do it.

'You want $10,000,000 to automate motor assembly!!!?'

'Yes.'

'But it's just a design, it's not proven. Suppose it doesn't work.'

'Then fire me.'

'And me,' added Brian the Design Director.

After a lot of sweaty reviews with the President of Europe, Genghis, and the European bean counters we got our $10 million, and it did work so I wasn't fired. We got a Queen's Award for Technology and a trip to Buckingham Palace for that one instead. To see the Queen, I took with me two shop floor workers whose names were drawn from a hat. They loved it. The Queen will never know what she did for our labour relations.

After our initial automation success, the capital financing doors were open and we brought in robots to palletise the finished product and unmanned forklift trucks to move our material about labour free. As the revolution progressed we relinquished more and more responsibility to the shop floor. Typically, the Safety Engineer went. In his place a Total Customer Service group took over responsibility for plant safety. They did better than the management had ever done and established an accident-free environment for year after year. I totally restructured the management team. I got rid of layer upon layer of managers and gave the best remaining streamlined structure total profit responsibility for their section, together with the means to run a profit centre. I had a rule of thumb with my managers. If you complain about another function enough and blame it for your shortfalls, you will end up running said department. It worked like a dream and soon the whole place was self co-ordinated and running like a Swiss watch. Such was our success that we soaked up five other European plants, one from Germany, and two from France and our own southern operations in Maidenhead and Harmondsworth and got a bit of a reputation as the Pac Man of B&D, chomping up other factories as we went. But our costs, quality and customer service were becoming legendary and we were irresistible.

I was very, very tired. There is a picture of me in 1988 in *Management Today*, and I look terrible. I couldn't help myself. Such was my enthusiasm for the company and the job in hand I drove myself onward day after day. On annual holidays in Tuscany, I would sleep for the first three days, usually in the shade of a cypress tree in the garden of the villa we stayed in in those days. It was all such good fun that I never thought to ease off.

In 1988, *Management Today* nominated us as one of the six best factories in Britain after an exhaustive visit to the plant and having taken Boston Consulting Group's advice. It was immensely gratifying and not a little flattering. Awards came thick and fast and I was invited to join the Great and the Good who advised the regional office of the Bank of England. They do superb dinners, the only price being you have to sing for your supper. I was very proud of my plant, and even more so of my gang of Geordies who made the whole thing tick and whirr so consistently and so well. From 2,700 people struggling to turn out 40,000 power tools per week and barely two new products per year, we were now turning out 235,000 power tools per week and ten new products per year, the big difference being, there were only 1,500 of us now. And I had the place under such tight control that the Internal Auditors and even the External Auditors were unable to find a single thing to criticise in their annual comprehensive sift through our nether regions, the first time this had ever happened. This was a two edged sword. The Board hated to pay auditors for a nil result even though they loved the result itself and even I liked to see something come out in the auditor's report with which I could improve the operations. Honestly! Some people are never satisfied! Revolution had been wrought.

CHAPTER 7

Politics and pandemonium

You ask me what my three priorities are.
My answer is Education, Education, Education.

Tony Blair 1997

IN 1983 THE LOCAL MP whose constituency the factory was in, retired. In his place a fresh faced, apparently pleasant young man, Tony Blair, had been elected. At the time the event passed relatively unnoticed, though the vast majority of the employees had trooped out in his support on polling day. You could put a monkey up for election in Sedgefield and so long as it had a notice saying 'Labour' round its neck, it would get elected, scattered as the constituency was by pit villages. Most of the employees were ex miners or their families. Three years on, I was stopped by one of the machine shop setters as I came into work. He wanted to talk with me urgently, he said. He was a Labour Party activist and sat on the Constituency Party Executive. He told me that there was big trouble brewing. The union members of the executive were pressing the new MP very hard to 'do something about the non Union Black and Decker' and he was afraid the MP would be forced to respond. It's a measure of how good our relationships were with the employees that I came by this information in the way I did. I thanked him and said, no, under no circumstances would our conversation be reported, and I would consider what to do.

I decided to invite the MP in for a day. After all, we were the biggest employer in his constituency and our employees were almost all constituents to a man. It was probably overdue that we formed some sort of business relationship. And in he bounced, devoting a whole day to the visit. Tony Blair was indeed as fresh faced as the election posters predicted, wholly unstuffy and potentially very charming. I sat him down in Eddie's office, neutral ground, and we told him what we were about. I resurrected my old inverted snobberies and told him that he should have no preconceptions about my or, indeed, Eddie's, politics. We were both working class lads made good, we had strong Union connections and I even quoted him my father's history as a Branch Secretary of the NUR. It was shameless, the old socialist game of 'my working class credentials are bigger than yours', but I would be damned if I was going to be told how to relate to my employees by a Fettes educated toff. We then told him all about our philosophies in managing people, of fairness, dignity, treating people as individuals, and we dwelt in detail on how we achieved this. We had a good story to tell by then. We told him about monthly briefings of the entire factory when I would address all the shifts through twenty-four hours on good news, bad news, prospects and plans and how those briefings were open to discussion at the end. We showed him the weekly newsletter published every Friday which consisted of one third gossip, one third company news and one third white propaganda. We told him of the 'Hotline', an internal telephone number that any employee could leave a question on or make a comment on anonymously with a guarantee that the question or comment would be printed in the next newsletter with my response. And we told him of the monthly 'Speak Out' sessions when I chose fifteen employees at random, gathered them in a conference room, symbolically locked the door and then commanded them to tell me exactly what they thought about the company, the plans and their treatment that month with a guarantee of anonymity and action. We rounded off this exposure of our methods by telling him that we had three main priorities in maintaining good employee relations:

Communication, Communication and Communication.

And a sound bite was born. We also told him how Christian names were universal throughout the organisation, not as some patronising gesture but because formality was the enemy of good communication. It seems he took that one on board too. I did tell you earlier of how creative Eddie was in human resource management.

We told him we were not anti Union, just non Union, and we preferred communicating with employees directly rather than through a Union with its inevitable Chinese whisper consequences and ideological slant.

Before lunch, I told him that I was taking him on a plant tour, during which he was free to approach anyone and everyone he chose, when I would withdraw to non hearing distance while he conducted his own surgery with his and my constituents. In other words, no hand picked management stooges. And he did, extensively, so that we were late for lunch. Lunch had been set up in the factory canteen and it told a story in itself. We only had the one canteen, for everybody, shop floor, management and distinguished visitors. When distinguished visitors were on the plant, and there were many, usually customer boards from all over Europe or politicians, we set up a table right in the centre of the big canteen with white tablecloths, silver service and employees serving. He commented on this and said he felt a little conspicuous with the special privileges of tablecloths and service, and I told him a story. I told him that a year or so before, I had had this brilliant idea. Eddie Jones had persuaded me to buy uniforms for all employees, smart grey slacks, T shirts or sweatshirts and grey jackets with the company logo on. My idea was that I would demonstrate my 'togetherness' by wearing the grey jacket at work, Japanese style, and I did. In less than a week, the messages came pouring in: 'Tell Dave to put his suit back on. We don't like our General Manager looking like that.' They had a very clear idea of who they wanted to be represented by and it wasn't by a little guy who looked just the same as them. It was the same with the special canteen service for distinguished guests. The employees would accept nothing less, I told him.

He was very relaxed by now and we had a very pleasant and uninhibited conversation over lunch. I told him candidly that irrespective of our politics, Margaret Thatcher's total dominance of British politics at the time was not good for democracy, and the Labour Party needed to sort itself out. I went further; I told him they could have no credibility while there were nutters like Arthur Scargill associated with their cause. Don't worry, he said, Scargill was sorted, he was a spent force. And he was right.

We concluded the day with a round-up meeting in my office where he told us that 'If all British companies were run like this, there would be no need for Unions. You will get no more problems with me or the constituency executive.' And he was true to his word. He might be Fettes educated, but he certainly wasn't an effete toff.

From that meeting, we met occasionally over the next few years. Annie met him at the Spennymoor Town Council Christmas Dinner and Ball, a gruesome rubber chicken event that we were always invited to and felt obliged to go to. I was the guest after-dinner speaker and sat on the top table with their other guest of honour,

Tony Blair. Annie had taken on her role as the first lady of Black and Decker Spennymoor with barely a grumble and she was brilliant at it. She had absolutely no inhibitions when dealing with dignitaries or even big time politicians, and this evening she was seated at the top table with Tony Blair on her left. I listened discreetly while she chatted to him.

'Are you married, Tony?'

'Yes, my wife Cherie couldn't make it today.'

'Does she go out to work?'

'Yeah, she's a barrister in London, that's why she's not here.'

'Any children?'

'Two boys, Euan and Nicky. Nicky's only a baby.'

'How does she manage to be a barrister with two young children?'

'Oh, we have a Nanny.'

'So you have a house in London and one up here and a Nanny?'

'Yeah.'

Then the killer question –

'Two houses, Nannies and barristers. What the hell are you doing in the Labour party, then?'

To his immense credit he gave her a thirty minute, impassioned speech on what he believed in and how that was totally in line with the Labour party of his vision.

'Sorry I asked,' said Annie.

Over the next few years, we alternated as guest speakers at the Spennymoor function. No one could say we lacked commitment to good causes. Annie became a favourite of the town council with her genuine down to earth approach, and they just loved her. She disappeared for an hour after one of the dinners and I eventually found her in the Mayoral Chair in the Council Chamber with the Mayor's full regalia round her neck, holding forth in great merry style to the assembled admiring Councillors. She was sorry when we had to go. Driving home we fell to discussing Tony Blair.

'With a bit of luck and a following wind, that guy will end up Leader of the Labour Party and even Prime Minister,' I said, little knowing in 1986 how right I was to be proved eleven years later. By then I was very impressed by him if not by his politics.

Then in 1987 I got a call from the Chairman one morning fresh in the office from my morning six-mile run. He said the Prime

Minister, Margaret Thatcher, wanted to come during an election tour of the North-East, but it was up to us to issue an invitation. Did I want the bother, and would it be all right with the employees, socialists almost to the last man. Did I! Eddie said the employees would love it and I told the Chairman to issue the invitation, hoping that Eddie was right and we wouldn't have embarrassing scenes.

In due course, the Agent for the North-East Conservative Party called me to make the arrangements. He told me that nobody must know she was coming, for security reasons, the Prime Minister still being a target of the IRA at that time. Also, the SAS and Special Branch would have to give the place the once-over a few days before the visit and sniffer dogs would have to inspect the whole factory just hours before the visit. Don't worry, he said, it will all be very discreet. Let me get this right, I said. A platoon of the SAS, and a collective noun of Special Branch together with sniffer dogs will descend on my factory, and I am not supposed to let anybody know there is something afoot? Discreet? DISCREET? That will be about as discreet as a pig in a synagogue! Don't worry, he said, it will all work out wonderfully well. He would come through himself and give me some advice on the visit and how to handle the press. And he did. He said there would be at least fifty pressmen with television cameras, microphones, the works. He said they would be animals, it was not unknown for them to fist fight one another for the best shot or sound bite. The best thing we could do is erect stands around the factory tour and keep them corralled in the stands. I didn't believe a word of it. That nice John Simpson couldn't possibly behave like that. He left me with more dilemmas than I had when he arrived. How not to tell anybody the Prime Minister was coming while entertaining the SAS, Special Branch and sniffer dogs and erecting grandstands around the plant. Maintaining secrecy seemed a big stretch to me. Ah well, hey ho, just get on with it, I thought. I made up stories about security inspections for safety's sake and 'better be safe than sorry these uncertain days' and other such tripe. On the eve of her visit, while the SAS were 'reconnoitring the terrain', a passing assembly shop girl confided, 'They're here for the Prime Minister, you know. She's coming tomorrow.' 'You may say that,' I said, 'I couldn't possibly comment.' I was really getting the hang of the Civil Service speak.

On the morning of the great day, all was ready. Lunch would be served in the Boardroom, and the Press would be fed in the conference room below. I was just waiting now to launch Margaret Thatcher on a less than surprised Spennymoor Black and Decker world. We got a call from the prospective Tory MP for Darlington. Could he join the tour with the Prime Minister? I took advice from the Tory party agent who said no, he could not, this was not his constituency. I passed this on to the enquirer who persisted all morning until I was fed up with him. He turned up anyway.

Eventually we got a call from the 'Battle Bus'. They were on their way. Could we possibly make sure there was whisky waiting their arrival? I told them this was a dry plant and no spirits were allowed on the premises. I had a thing about drinking on factory premises after my Glasgow experiences and the penalty was instant dismissal if you brought drink onto the plant. But still they persisted. I got another call five minutes later with the same request. I told them no again. Then another call, same thing again. This time I told them in no uncertain terms there would be no drinks on arrival and they gave up.

When she arrived, it was with Dennis, of course, and a horde of pressmen disgorged from a following coach. We went inside and I introduced her to my management team. 'Best management team outside your cabinet, Prime Minister,' I said, and they all preened. Judging by some of her later thoughts about her cabinet, I was probably doing my team a disservice. We put the pressmen in the conference room for their lunch and retired to the boardroom for lunch with the Prime Minister and her entourage. 'Where are the press?' she enquired of her secretary, 'I hope we are not feeding them as well!' I told her that not being one to get on the wrong side of the fourth estate, we were feeding them with a rather good buffet on the floor below. She wanted to know about the company and the factory and our philosophies in managing people and we had an easy and good discussion. I told her this would be followed by a factory tour when she could interact with the voters.

'Right!' she said, 'come on, you lot, we're going!' and we trooped out down the stairs to begin the tour. Passing the conference room below the pressmen suddenly saw her heading for the tour and immediately threw their food and plates to the ground, trampling them into the carpet as they rushed after her, fearful of losing a good sound bite. In the machine shop at the start of the tour, two lone setters stood, arms folded across their chests glowering at her as if daring her to speak to them. She spotted them and without a word left our carefully prepared tour route and headed purposefully thirty yards across the machine shop to confront what were obviously challenges to her politics and even her personage. A look of initial surprise came across the setters' faces, followed rapidly by horror. They couldn't retreat; they would have to be bearded by the strident Prime Minister. She had them eating out of her hand in thirty seconds before striding back to me and our tour route. Pandemonium reigned from then on as we processed through the plant. I had told the manufacturing supervisors that when a certain personage appeared on the plant, they could release their charges from their work to come and see. The agent had been right, the press were, if not animals, then thugs, mainly with one another as they fought for the best shot and comment, though I like to remember that the nice John Simpson stood a little aloof from the scrum. Employees flocked to the Prime Minister. Any fears of embarrassing scenes were quickly dispelled. 'Maggie, Maggie! Look o'er 'ere while I get a photo,' they shouted and she obliged them liberally. 'Did you get your shot, dear? Come over here so you can get a good one, dear,' she said to them over and over again as she disdained the security barriers and Special Branch to drag surprised but happy snappers into the mêlée. The Special Branch man didn't look nearly so happy. The press continued their bad tempered coverage.

'Get out of the way, you're in my shot. It's not about you, it's about the Prime Minister,' shouted a particularly belligerent cameraman.

'Don't move,' commanded the Tory agent, 'it's your bloody factory; you can stand where you like.' Right now it didn't seem like my factory at all.

On it went in similar fashion until, at last, it was over and time for the Prime Minister to go to her next appointment. I made the nine o'clock news that evening, not for anything I did or said, but just as the grey suit trotting by a resplendent Prime Minister who was savagely berating a BBC newsman for daring to ask about unemployment in the North-East. 'You only ever want to talk about bad news! What about this magnificent factory employing thousands since 1965? Why don't you ask me about that?' she berated him. He was perfectly happy having got a question and a raging answer to fill a few seconds on that evening's news. Annie presented her with a bouquet, and she was off in her Battle Bus, the press in hot pursuit. It suddenly seemed very, very quiet, and the factory was mine again.

Reading the political analysis pages after the election, I learned that that day had become known as 'Wobbly Thursday' because the opinion polls were indicating a fall off of support, and in any case, Margaret Thatcher had a raging toothache with no time to get it attended to. I was sorry then that I hadn't foregone my principles. Sorry about the whisky, Lady Thatcher.

CHAPTER 8

European adventures

To enter Europe, you must have a valid passport with a
photograph of yourself in which you look like you are
being booked on charges of soliciting sheep.

Dave Barry

B Y 1989, ROGER, THE REMARKABLE General Manager, had ascended
to Europe as President, and he was ready to make some big
changes. Ever since Europe had been colonised by Black and Decker
many years before from its initial base in Maidenhead, England, each
national European country had been a fiefdom with its own
Managing Director, manufacturing plant and design centre. In the
years of colonisation this had been a very smart move. The European
national markets were markedly different at the outset and it made
sense to design, make and sell products from within in order to create
a market. But times had changed. There was now wide homogeneity
in the various markets as far as products were concerned, but the
national design centres continued to design and develop products in
competition with one another and the fiefdoms had become feudal
baronies as they competed to grab a bigger share of the manufacturing
load for their voracious factories. This nonsense was compounded by
a world wide movement toward globalisation driven by the Japanese
and Americans. We were wasting precious new product development
and capital resources by wholesale duplication across Europe, and the
individual companies expended at least as much energy fighting each
other as in fighting the competition. It had to stop. Roger ripped the
various manufacturing plants and the Design Centres away from the
feudal Barons and combined them into a European entity rather than
a national. There was furore as each of the national Managing
Directors saw their jobs suddenly reduced to managing sales and
marketing companies, and under strict European direction. I don't
know how Roger did it, but the furore died down and the national
Managing Directors got on with restructuring Europe to fight the
competition on the Sales and Marketing front. I was appointed to run
European Manufacturing and Product Development with three plants

in Italy, one in Switzerland, two in Germany and the super plant in County Durham. I was now in Europe.

I maintained an office in Spennymoor and travelled out from there to my various outposts. It was very hard work, converting Germans, Swiss, Italians and Brits into a single entity with a common objective, especially since they all had different finance and computer systems and a long history of antagonism and I laboured mightily to achieve it. This meant that Annie and the family barely saw me from Sunday night to Friday evening since I was travelling so much and sleeping when I wasn't travelling. British Midland who flew from Teesside even featured me in an advertising campaign, such was the custom I put their way. The advert ran in the national press and a cutting from the *Daily Telegraph* eventually found its way back to my desk with some demeaning but funny comments on it from the Spennymoor wags. The brilliant Annie accepted it all and got on with maintaining the home front with her usual cheerful competence.

Slowly, slowly I made progress. The plants were all assigned a product profile at which they were to excel, instead of trying to be all things for their Feudal Baron chief, and I had got common systems in place with all the plants now measurable against each other by the same Management Accounting system. And I had got product cost if not under control, then at least free of the wilder, eccentric Italian variations that had been a feature of the past. Our financial results were improving rapidly, some payback to the feudal barons for the loss of their manufacturing influence, and everyone was happy with progress. Then we got a new world wide president.

Mike was a giant of a man in both physical stature and business ability and he was the only American I ever met who was truly international in his outlook. He had come from the automobile industry with Ford and Chrysler and had worked for them all over the world. I liked him immensely from the first meeting as he set about stamping his unique authority on Black and Decker world wide. We had what I like to think was a unique relationship. I told him exactly what I thought because I thought he deserved to hear it and he always listened, though he sometimes did as he originally intended, unspoilt by my blunt Yorkshire analysis. The relationship is most closely defined by Robert Townsend in his marvellous book *Up the Organisation* in which he recounts a story from his own self effacing experience:

To increase our share of the market a few years ago, I was on the verge of approving the start-up of a new subsidiary – which would compete with our bread-and-butter business – at discount prices. To verify my own brilliance I tried the idea out on a tall, rangy regional vice-president named Stepnowski. After hearing the plan described in some detail, he sank the whole project with one sentence: 'I don't know what you call it, but we Polacks call that "pissing in the soup".'

I sometimes had to tell Mike he was 'pissing in the soup' and he appreciated the candour even when he didn't agree.

Mike wanted a European Board to counter the potentially overwhelming American influence in the rapidly advancing globalisation of the company and Roger agreed. And so it was that I became European Vice President for Manufacturing and Product Development on the newly formed European Board under Roger's Chairmanship and Presidency. Roger insisted that as a European Director I should relocate my office to the European headquarters in Slough and establish a domicile down there. Annie and I talked this over and easily agreed that moving the family from their home and schools at this stage was unthinkable so we bought a really nice two bed-roomed apartment in Farnham Royal on the golf course where I could live during the working week. My routine then became: up at 4.30 a.m. Mondays, commuter flight to Heathrow and onward to either Slough head office or deepest, darkest Europe depending on my diary. Annie would not see me again until late Friday evenings. It was bloody hard work for all of us but immensely satisfying for all that. My travel became so routine that we never discussed upcoming destinations in our leisure weekends, so that when I called home on a Monday evening, Annie would ask where I was. Baltimore, I would reply, or Frankfurt or Milan or Lyon or Singapore or . . . It really could have been anywhere.

With the travelling went the bonuses of foreign cultures and especially foreign foods. I tended to stay where there were excellent restaurants either in-house or nearby. I even stayed at one hotel in Italy regularly even though the rooms were miniscule and basic because it had a wonderful restaurant. My team and I would generally arrive late in the evening courtesy of British Airways after an exhausting day's work back in Slough and even late, the restaurant would welcome us warmly.

'I see there is a new item on your menu, Mario. What is *puledro*, some kind of chicken?'

'No, no Signor! Is not chicken. Is horse!'

'Aargh!' (collectively from the English team).

'No, no! Is OK. Is small horse!'

I had 'small horse' while my team looked on in irrational disgust. It was delicious.

Increasingly I was being pulled into global debates and meetings and life got even more frenzied with all the intercontinental travel on top of the European travel. Typically, on Annie's 50th birthday, Julie, our daughter, had organised a surprise party at her house in a marquee to be erected in her back garden. Since she lived next door but one, maintaining surprise would be difficult with an enormous tent in the garden, so the arrangement was that I would whisk Annie away to the very swish Sharrow Bay Hotel on Ullswater on Friday, when the tent erectors would move in and have it ready for Saturday's party. There was only one problem. I was in Singapore that week for a global meeting. The meeting finished late on Thursday, and I caught the 11.00 p.m. flight for London, arriving at 05.00 a.m. on Friday. Then I drove up to County Durham and did my whisking away. We had a wonderful stay and dinner at the Sharrow Bay, without me falling asleep in my soup, and I delivered Annie back to Dalton Piercy for 2.00 p.m. on Saturday where we had a wonderful surprise party with all of our friends from worldwide. On the following Monday I flew out to Hong Kong for another round of meetings. Frantic or what?

Meanwhile, the giant Mike was intent on making changes to product development to turn it into a truly global process, and this meant massive retraining right across the Corporation at all levels. A week long course was eventually devised through which every single person remotely connected to product development right across the Corporation was to be retrained in the newly defined, global process. It would take a year of intensive training with one course being run each month, alternating in location between Europe and America. Mike insisted the courses be run by the Vice Presidents themselves to give the initiative real credibility. He was right. Without the Vice Presidents' demonstrated commitment, nobody would believe the Corporation meant business. So every month I had to block out one whole week to lead the training in what was an overstuffed diary already. Somehow, I and my US counterparts carried it through – but I was getting ominously tired.

While all this was going on, Mike and Roger, World and European Presidents respectively, decided we were now ready for the ultimate change in organisational structure and assigned a Product Group Leader for all the parts of our vast range of products. They would have global strategic responsibility for their product group and its development. The last step in this massive change would be to give the Product Group Leaders the manufacturing and design resources to carry through their strategies. But we weren't ready for that yet.

Toward the end of that training year, I got some very bad news while running one of the courses. Mike had had a very big bust up with the Chairman and Chief Executive Officer, and he was leaving. I was distraught. He had brought true global vision to the corporation for the first time as far as I was concerned, and just as we were embarked on the very delicate and intricate manoeuvre of transforming disparate global fiefdoms into a truly international commercial fighting force, the prime driver was going. Bugger, bugger, bugger!

We threw him and his charming wife a great farewell dinner party at Cliveden where Annie and I slept in the converted billiard room where Winston Churchill had once played billiards after dinner with the Astors. We roasted Mike unmercifully after dinner but with great and obvious affection and he was much moved.

CHAPTER 9

The end game

To Shakespeare, in the eyes of heaven,
The Ages of a Man are seven;
But businessmen, it's clear to me,
Are limited, at best, to three.

Bertie Ramsbottom: 'The Ages of Man'

from *The Bottom Line*

B EFORE THE GLOBAL PRESIDENT MIKE left he had completed his
world wide reorganisation. Parts of it came as a surprise to me.
He appointed General Managers responsible for product groups across
Europe. I had been party to the discussions that led up to this and I
was wholeheartedly behind it. It was the obvious next step and I
could also see it as an early way out of the organisation and into my
own ambitions. I had long held the view that I wanted out at fifty,
but it never appeared practical or financially possible. My view was
based on how tired I had got, and that running international
manufacturing plants was a younger man's game anyway, not to
mention my more selfish motives of detailed plans for my retirement.
The last piece of the reorganisation was to be the assignment of
manufacturing plants and design centres associated with their product
groups. I didn't believe the candidates were ready for that yet, all of
them being commercial types and marketeers. I envisaged a steady
hand-over during which I would train them in the technical
mysteries of Manufacturing and Product Development. And that was
the plan until the last minute. A day's conference had been organised
to launch the new organisation onto a startled European company.
All the key players from across Europe were there to hear of the
revolution and I was to take a major role in leading the conference.
At the last minute, I looked at the organisation structure provided and
discovered to my immense surprise that Manufacturing and Product
Development were to be reassigned straight away. I wasn't dismayed
or upset about it, just surprised by the expeditiousness of it. My
usually reliable political antennae had not picked this up and neither
Roger nor Mike had mentioned it. I went in search of my 'sources'

172

who told me the story. Apparently one of the candidates for the Product General Manager role, a brash young marketing thruster, had dug his heels in and refused the job unless it had manufacturing and the design centre with it. Mike and Roger had succumbed to the pressure and changed the plan. They were obviously ashamed to tell me. Hey ho, on with the motley, I thought. It suited my plans though I felt even more strongly that the brash young chap was the least equipped of all of them to handle the breadth of the new role. I got stuck into the launch conference with a gusto that couldn't be mistaken for anything other than wholehearted support. I had the last spot of the day and I had organised it so that with the full knowledge of the new organisational structure by the end of the day, the European team would be sent in focus groups to brainstorm the difficulties they would face in implementing the structure. I would facilitate their responses and round up the whole day sending them off massively enthusiastic and full of piss and vinegar for the task ahead. That was the theory. In facilitating the session and setting up the task for their task groups, I couldn't resist a last massive dig at the young upstart marketer and soon-to-be global Business Unit Manager and I used a long shaggy dog story to do both jobs. The story went like this.

Don't imagine that this will be easy. There are longstanding attitudes, biases and even animosities between Marketing, Manufacturing and Product Development that will have to be overcome. Take young Charles here [the brash young marketer]. This weekend he faces some very tough initial decisions that will influence how the organisation at large views his positioning, and on that will depend his credibility. Where will he base his head office for example? His decision will send messages to the organisation whether he likes it or not. Will he base it in Germany, a key market? Or will it be in Slough, the historic, if distant, centre for European management? Or will it be at the Manufacturing Plant in Spennymoor? On this decision will rest how the organisation views his bias and it is vital to get it right. I can just picture the scene over the weekend while Charles wrestles with this dilemma and it will go something like this:

Charles paced the floor mulling over his choices for head office location. His wife had dinner ready but so engrossed in his dilemma was he that dinner was foregone and he paced on, wracking his brains for the right answer. All Saturday night he worried and fretted but he just couldn't decide. No sooner had he decided on one location than one of the other two came to mind with their claims to his patronage. On and on he worried into the early hours of the morning. Then just as dawn was breaking, the clouds opened and a beam of brilliant white light shone down on poor Charles and a commanding voice said, 'Have faith, my son. Go to Spennymoor!' But Charles thought little of it other than as a hallucination brought on by his utter weariness, and he worried on and on throughout the day. Just before sunset, the clouds parted again, the beam of brilliant bright light shone down on him again and the voice commanded, 'HAVE FAITH, MY SON. GO TO SPENNYMOOR!' This time Charles could not ignore it and he made up his mind. 'I WILL go to Spennymoor!' he said, his mind now clear and made up. He slept well and on Monday morning drove up to Spennymoor full of enthusiasm and vigour for the task ahead, all worries now lifted from his shoulders. He parked his car and walked, whistling, over to the factory and stepped into the hallowed halls of Spennymoor – straight in front of a passing fork lift truck speeding parts to the drill line. Poor Charles, he had two broken arms, two broken legs and a severely bruised ego as he lay there unconscious on the ground. Then the clouds parted and a brilliant white light shone down on this bloody mess and the voice said, 'MARKETING BASTARD!'

The conference erupted in uncontrollable laughter and even Charles laughed with it. He didn't really have much choice. I then told the gathering that with attitudes like that throughout the organisation, I needed their help and advice in overcoming them in the upcoming reorganisation. Their final task of the day was to consider this in their focus groups and report back in half an hour. The delegates then went away in good spirits and the new organisation was born.

In the following weeks, Mike and Roger broke cover and Mike told me what they wanted me to do. As well as keeping an eye on Manufacturing, now in the hands of the marketing general managers, they wanted me to do a strategic study. Industrial China was stirring and already making big waves in the world market for power tools with exceedingly cheap imports sold by cowboy traders across Europe and the USA. The product wasn't much good but at the price it was a really good mug's eyeful. Clearly we had to have a strategy for dealing with the emerging giant and Mike wanted me to spend the next year studying the problem, close up and personal, and come up with a strategy. I was massively enthusiastic. It was a great strategic threat and I couldn't wait to get my teeth into it. It was then that Mike left after his bust up with the CEO, though my remit was maintained.

His replacement as Corporate President was an American I knew well with a sales and marketing background. It was ever thus in the Corporate thinking. He turned out to be a bit of a damp squib in the bigger role and worse, he had little or no time at all for the technical side of the business. In fact, he was totally dismissive of manufacturing as a strategic strength and treated it as an unfortunately necessary irritant. Nevertheless, he formed a Global Operating Board with the technical functions represented by myself and my US equivalent and we began to do some good work on a global basis rather than a regional European, American or South-East Asia basis. It was long overdue. One of the first discussions was around the South-East Asian region which was becoming more and more important as China grew. The South-East Asian tigers were stirring in a big way. It was resolved at the Global Operating Board that we needed to significantly strengthen the organisation out there, and it put an extra emphasis on the China study I was doing.

Ominously, the CEO had appointed a 'Manufacturing Specialist' reporting directly to him to advise on manufacturing issues. He was a Neanderthal straight out of the 1950s 'What's good for America is good for the world' mode and was widely despised for it inside and outside the US operations. The worrying thing was that he had the all powerful CEO's ear. The Global Operating Board fell to discussing whether he should be invited to join the board. After a lot of debate, much of it negative, I told them that 'I would rather have him inside the tent pissing out than outside the tent pissing in.' The President rebuked me on my colourful phrase and I had to tell him that I had lifted it from an American President, Lyndon Baines Johnson no less, referring to J. Edgar Hoover. Colourful or not it carried the day and the Neanderthal joined the board where we could keep an eye on him.

The next year was a whirlwind of travel in and out of South-East Asia with crazy itineraries. I travelled extensively in mainland China – Chengdu, Shanghai and Shenzen I remember, and of course Hong Kong and after six months was ready with my strategic recommendations. I won't bore you with the detail, but the two key recommendations were first that we needed a much stronger presence in the Far East and in China in particular and second that we must have a joint manufacturing venture inside China, both being well overdue and critical to the future. It was agreed and I was commissioned to find a Chinese joint venture partner, and off I went again. We didn't have a good record with joint ventures, paying them far too little attention in the past, so I decided on an excellent Hong Kong based company with factories up in mainland China and negotiated heads of agreement with them. They were enthusiastic to be associated with such a big brand name but they were a family business of immense proportions and they had their own ideas about how the joint venture would work, so negotiations could be difficult at times. After a lot of to-ing and fro-ing we eventually agreed the principles and our CEO, no less, came out to Hong Kong to sign the joint Letter of Intent. My job was done. The detailed legal agreement was to be negotiated with the South-East Asian group.

Then I heard something on my US political grapevine. Roger, the European President, was to be sent out to Singapore as the new President South-East Asia as part of the strengthening up we had recommended. The only trouble was, he didn't know. I told him what I had learned and he replied that it was totally wrong as he knew who was going. I had to tell him that the man he thought was going had in fact eventually turned the job down and was leaving the company as a result. He didn't believe me. Two days later he was ordered out to Singapore with no choices. He was going whether he liked it or not. I told him he was just the man to take on what was a massive challenge and strategically, China deserved no less. He eventually went in good heart and it was he who finally completed the legal negotiations with the Chinese joint venture partner. I was totally content now with the job I had done in the Far East. There were overtures to go out and join the new South-East Asian organisation, but I had already decided I was going. I was very tired and all the signs were that the Americans were coming to reclaim the European Company for their very own as part of the advancing globalisation. As far as I was concerned, the Barbarians were at the gates of Europe and I wanted no part of that coming débâcle. I told the company early and firmly that I was retiring. The most senior Americans were not disappointed.

Before leaving, I had one last task, to look at the emerging East European and Russian markets with the objective of picking up new technologies and low cost sources of parts and manufacturing. The Soviet economic empire, if there had ever been one, had collapsed, and with it the satellite country's economies. With the economic collapse came the fall of the Iron Curtain and the rise of *glasnost*, all of which resulted in astounding accessibility to their manufacturing and even research resources, suddenly without finance or purpose. Typical was an approach to us by the former nuclear research facility of the Soviet Union, who, in common with all the state industries, secret or not, were now seeking a new purpose and even survival in life by selling their expertise in the global markets. This particular organisation claimed to have developed a new motor which they anticipated would revolutionise power tools and I met them in Moscow. They had excellent technical credentials but were almost paranoid in their secretiveness about their invention, as they had been conditioned to be by years of Soviet government. Nevertheless, they invited us to their research facility behind the Urals in order to advance the debate and establish their technical credibility. The Russians always put their sensitive installations behind the Urals, I was to discover, the mountains representing a great barrier to western invasion in the Russian mind, though I doubt whether an American Intercontinental Ballistic Missile would have found the Urals much of an obstruction.

If they were paranoid about their motor invention, they certainly weren't about their facility. They presented me with a glossy sales brochure, no doubt designed and put together by the Moscow State University marketing faculty judging by its utter ineptness. It began promisingly enough. There were colour pictures of beautiful country-side and lakes surrounding their research centre and quite explicit descriptions of their role in developing the USSR's nuclear capability over many years. It went downhill from there. The brochure went on to explain at gruesome length that unfortunately, even with this towering technological resource, they had managed to pollute that same green land and the lakes in the pictures above, over many miles radius, with atomic radiation. The land itself was seriously radio-active. On the plus side though, they were intending to put all their profits into cleaning up their mess, the brochure said. So even though the research facility could not be found on any map I consulted, it probably glowed in the dark and would be easy to find. I declined their kind invitation to visit. One of my senior technical men who was much braver than I and intrigued by their potential technical expertise made the trip instead. I insisted he carry a radiation meter with him and if, or when, it approached danger levels, he was to remove himself immediately.

After the visit he reported that they were indeed genuine and that they possibly had something in their motor. As ever though, their paranoia had prevented any proper disclosure of the motor's technology. Eventually, after a visit to my research facilities and uninhibited disclosure of our detailed motor capabilities, they agreed that brilliant as their motor concept was, it could not compete with ours, and they went away.

This was typical of my Russian experiences, often very sad, sometimes even frightening but by and large disappointing and unproductive. Russia and its old satellites were a terrible mess and the ordinary people were suffering the most, as ever. In Moscow I met a member of the Russian State Symphony Orchestra, a violinist, who was playing solo in the restaurant where we ate. He played beautifully and with a very high quality instrument and was reduced to this because none of the state employees were being paid, and, as he said to me, he had to feed his family. Similarly, the door of the restaurant was guarded by two Russian paratroopers in full kit with their Kalashnikovs. They weren't being paid by the state either and so earned a living moonlighting as doormen in what was then a very dangerous city.

I concluded my work was done and that Mother Russia or its Eastern European satellites had nothing to offer until after some considerable evolution, and I resolved to go.

In August 1995, I left after an uproarious party thrown by the Spennymoor factory, a valedictory tour of the European operations and a super dinner at the French Horn in Sonning thrown me by my European Board colleagues. My friends across the world sent me some very kind letters. Apparently it had come as a surprise to some and they suspected plots that didn't exist.

I was now a free man of my own free will. I was proud and happy at all the things achieved on my watch. I knew I would miss the male camaraderie of a tight management team and all my employee friends, but very happy, nevertheless, to contemplate a life outside Black and Decker.

'We'll do some world travelling of our own now,' I said to Annie. 'And I'm going to write a book.' And we did, but that's another story.